DEALING
WITH
DIFFICULT
CUSTOMERS

How to Turn Demanding, Dissatisfied, and
Disagreeable Clients Into Your Best Customers

DEALING

WITH

DIFFICULT

CUSTOMERS

NOAH FLEMING and **SHAWN VELTMAN**

CAREER
PRESS

Wayne, N.J.

DEALING WITH DIFFICULT CUSTOMERS
Edited by Roger Sheety
Typeset by Kara Kumpel
Cover design by Rob Johnson/toprotype
Cover illustration by Oakozhan/shutterstock
Printed in the U.S.A.

To order this title, please call toll-free 1-800-CAREER-1 (NJ and Canada: 201-848-0310) to order using VISA or MasterCard, or for further information on books from Career Press.

CAREER
PRESS

The Career Press, Inc.
12 Parish Drive
Wayne, NJ 07470
www.careerpress.com

Library of Congress Cataloging-in-Publication Data

Fleming, Noah, author. | Veltman, Shawn, author.
    Dealing with difficult customers : how to turn demanding, dissatisfied, and disagreeable clients into your best customers / Noah Fleming, Shawn Veltman.
    Wayne : Career Press, 2017. | Includes bibliographical references and index.
    LCCN 2017035957 (print) | LCCN 2017037756 (ebook) |
    ISBN 9781632658890 (ebook) | ISBN 9781632651174 (paperback)
    LCSH: Customer relations. | BISAC: BUSINESS & ECO-NOMICS
Customer Relations.

LCC HF5415.5 (ebook) | LCC HF5415.5 .F583 2017 (print) | DDC 658.8/12--dc23

LC record available at https://lccn.loc.gov/2017035957

MAR 1 5 2018

Contents

Part II

Part III

Foreword

I am a woman of the old school. I enjoy communication, human interaction, and I value great service. Whether it is in a restaurant, a retail store, a spa, a hotel or any service related industry for that matter, I always want to feel that someone took the time to appreciate my business and made a difference for me. The expectations I have might seem excessive to some, but after 35 years in fashion and retail, I am more convinced than ever that it's the attention to detail and our ability to create great experiences that have allowed companies to thrive in today's environment.

Noah and Shawn's book is an important reminder of all the little things that have impact. It's not about a deal or a freebie. Memorable experiences are the reasons a customer will continue to come back to you over and over. I realized there are so many opportunities for companies to succeed if they follow the human touch and get back to the basics. Too many companies focus on big changes, but in my view the most impactful improvements are created by doing just the opposite. Noah and Shawn stress the importance of creating simple but *consistent* steps to create a memorable customer experience. If you can get that right, you'll spend a lot less time "dealing" with difficult customers. Instead, they'll be thrilled—and lucky—to be doing business with you.

What makes a certain airline, hotel, restaurant, or a retail store stand out from the rest? It's the friendly greeting from a flight attendant. It's a water bottle as you wait in a line. It's a concierge who takes the time to make a recommendation based on your interests rather than his own; a waiter who is excited about the food they are about to serve you, or a personal follow-up call or thank you note from a sales associate after a purchase. All these little things make a difference. This is exactly the approach that they describe in the book, giving fantastic guidelines and hard-won insights to ensure that these changes will take hold in any company.

Noah and Shawn tell us to slow down selling and get to know the customer—take small measures and make decisions to do things consistently. That is how you'll see significant results. That is where real growth comes from. It seems so obvious, yet today we are moving so fast that we leave out the gestures that can make a difference.

I've seen these principles at work during my career, and I know that they are more important than ever today. This book is filled with tactics and strategies to help you realize these goals, and to create truly memorable experiences for your customers.

Word of mouth and testimonials are even more important today than ever before. In a global marketplace, it's almost impossible to compete on price, or on information, or on inventory. Instead, you need to find a way to compete on experience, on creating connections. You need to demonstrate to anybody who walks in that you have their best interest at heart, and that you'll do everything you can to truly understand what they want, what they need, and how they can get it in the easiest, most enjoyable way possible. The shift into digital, e-commerce, and social media make the pages that follow incredibly relevant as everyone understands how these areas have disrupted everything. Can we rethink the role of the retail store or other disrupted industries? Of course we can.

If you want to lie down and fall as a victim of change, then stay right where you are and stop reading right now. Or, if you want to thrive for many years to come, keep reading. These guys will show you the light.

Debra Margles
President of Michael Kors Canada
and lover of great experiences

Introduction

"They should not allow topless sunbathing on the beach. It was very distracting for my husband who just wanted to relax."

"We went on holiday to Spain and had a problem with the taxi drivers, as they were all Spanish."

"We booked an excursion to a water park, but no one told us we had to bring our own swimsuits and towels. We assumed it would be included in the price."

"We found the sand was not like the sand in the brochure. Your brochure shows the sand as white, but it was more yellow."

"No one told us there would be fish in the water. The children were scared."

"Although the brochure said there was a fully equipped kitchen, there was no egg-slicer in the drawers."

"I think it should be explained in the brochure that the local convenience store does not sell proper biscuits, like custard creams or ginger nuts."

"I compared the size of our one-bedroom suite to our friends' three-bedroom and ours was significantly smaller."

"I was bitten by a mosquito. The brochure did not mention mosquitoes."

"My fiancée and I requested twin beds when we booked, but instead we were placed in a room with a king bed. We now hold you responsible and want to be re-reimbursed for the fact that I became pregnant. This would not have happened if you had put us in the room that we booked."

As crazy as those previous 10 comments sound, they're all 100 percent real.[1] What they show us is the customer is obviously not always right. In fact, the customer is often blatantly wrong. Customers can be difficult. They can be a giant pain in the rear. And they can be utterly ridiculous at times. Of course, as the great Peter Drucker once said, "Without a customer, there is no business. A business exists to serve a customer."[2] This creates an interesting dynamic.

Now, this is not to imply that all customers are difficult, demanding, or irrational. In fact, we consistently find that the stories about the craziest customers are often passed down through time, exaggerated for effect, and overestimated as the reason for difficult interactions between customers and your company representatives.

In this book, we'll be sharing what we've learned about the reasons some customers are so hard to deal with, and what you can do to not only handle the difficult interactions, but to prepare yourself for them so well that you can avoid them altogether.

Before going any further, a little bit about us.

Noah Fleming: I'm an expert in all areas of customer relations. This includes sales, marketing, and customer service. I started consulting 15 years ago with smaller companies doing a few million in revenue to now working with major brands and organizations doing more than $5 billion in annual revenue. Shawn, who you'll hear from in a moment, has been working with me for years, behind the scenes, on some of my most important work. I've written two Amazon #1 best-selling books in the categories of sales, marketing, and customer service, including *Evergreen: Cultivate The Enduring Customer Loyalty That Keeps Your Business Thriving* and *The Customer Loyalty Loop: The Science Behind Creating Great Experiences and Lasting Impressions.* I routinely speak at major events such as SXSW (South by Southwest), Hubspot's Inbound, and numerous professional trade association meetings. I also write a free weekly newsletter called the *Tuesday Tidbit,* read by more than

30,000 readers. You can sign up for it on my website, NoahFleming.com. I live in Kingsville, Ontario with my wife, Heather, and our two girls, Avalon and Ella.

Shawn Veltman: For the past 15 years, I've been working with Noah to develop unique intellectual property, tools, and applications that Noah's firm, Fleming Consulting & Co., has successfully implemented in hundreds of companies across dozens of industries. I've been involved with a variety of companies, ranging from Internet start-ups to medical device manufacturers, helping executives envision and create the tools they need to get world-class performance from their sales and marketing teams. I recently married my wonderful wife, Marla, and we live in Calgary, Alberta.

The book has been written from both of our perspectives during many late-night Skype calls and long writing sessions. Throughout the book, you'll be hearing things from the perspective of "I," and in other cases, "we." If a comment or opinion is specifically Noah's or Shawn's, we've tried to highlight that fact, but for the majority of the book, you can consider the "I" or the "we" to be viewed as the collective "us."

We don't always agree on everything, but we're in full agreement on nearly everything written in this book. We've both seen how the tools and information contained in the pages that follow can have a dramatic impact on an organization's success. This book represents a collaboration of writing, but also our collaboration of working with clients together and separately during the past 12–15 years.

Let's get started!

Part I

Chapter 1

Defining the Difficult Customer

In the summer of 1954, a bus pulled up to a gorgeous 200-acre Boy Scout camp located in Oklahoma's Robbers Cave State Park, and 11 young campers quickly headed for the cabin they would share for the next three weeks.

The boys had all just finished 5th grade, and had been invited to the camp in part because they shared many similarities. They had above-average IQs, they had all received above-average marks in their classes the previous year, and they were all from two-parent, Protestant homes. Whenever I picture the scene in my mind, I can almost hear the *Leave It to Beaver* theme song as I imagine them running off the bus and toward their cabin on that first day.

During the next week, the boys would bond while taking part in summer camp activities that have remained largely unchanged through the last 100 years or so. They went on hikes through the gorgeous forest area that surrounded the camp, took advantage of the lake to go swimming and canoeing, and got to spend many afternoons playing baseball at a diamond provided by the camp. In the evening, they sat around the bonfire and shared stories with their camp counselors.

As happens at almost every summer camp, these boys who were strangers on the bus quickly became friends and created their own social structure. Leaders asserted themselves, outsiders could very quickly identify the high- and low-status members of the group, and they even began to form their own in-group customs and rules. In a move that is familiar to anybody who has watched one of the dozens of seasons of the popular television show *Survivor*, they even created their own group name ("The Eagles") and designed a flag to represent their new tribe.

The only difference between this group and thousands of other summer camps is the camp counselors were not there to ensure the group had the best time possible.

These counselors were, in fact, psychology researchers who were studying what would later become known as *Realistic Conflict Theory.*[1] In short, they wanted to find out two things:

1. How hard would it be to create intense animosity between people who are, in almost every respect, extremely similar?

2. Once that animosity has been created, how hard would it be to make them cooperate and maybe even like each other again?

Near the end of their first week at camp, the boys started to see clues that they weren't the only ones in their specific area. They saw signs that another group had being playing baseball in their diamond, swimming in their lake, and having the sheer audacity to be non-Eagles!

Clearly, this type of behavior could not stand. The boys knew they had to protect their precious diamond, to stake their claim on it, and so they planted their flag in the pitcher's mound of the baseball diamond when they weren't using it as a clear sign to anybody else that they were not welcome.

It's at this point in the experiment where the researchers got to unleash their inner pranksters, as they let the Eagles know that there was indeed another group sharing the camp with them. This other group, who had named themselves the Rattlers, had gone through exactly the same bonding experiences with each other that the Eagles had during the previous week.

Now, the researchers told each group that they were going to pit them against each other in a tournament of different camp activities: tent pitching, tug of war, baseball, touch football, and a scavenger hunt. The winners would receive a trophy, medals, and highly desirable pocket knives—a veritable treasure for the preteen boys in each group. For the researchers, the goal was to see how the groups of boys behaved toward each other. For the boys, it was a much more serious matter.

The name-calling began in the very first game. Not long after that, the Eagles burned their rivals' flag. The Rattlers retaliated by burning the Eagles' flag, which led to a nighttime raid of the Rattlers' cabin, where the Eagles stole the other campers' clothing and comic books, while ransacking the cabin.

Counter raids were executed, and the boys started walking around with large sticks and rocks in socks in case they needed to defend themselves from the rival group. At more than one point, the researchers had to step in to stop fights from breaking out among the groups. It became a real-life version of the classic *Lord of the Flies* story.

In short, the answer to the researchers' first question about how easy it would be to turn two groups against each other seemed to be, "disturbingly easy."[2]

The final part of the experiment, that of reconciling the two groups, was much less successful and much harder than turning them against each other in the first place. We'll examine how they did it shortly, but first we want to examine why this is such an important study, and what new research shows us about the way that groups turn on each other.

It Is Not Enough That I Succeed—Others Must Fail

The Robbers Cave study is perhaps the most famous piece of research in all social psychology. It is an extremely succinct look at how easy it is for groups to bond together, and especially for groups to label others as outsiders (and therefore, enemies).

Remember, the two groups of boys mentioned moments ago were picked because they were so similar. They were matched randomly, but within a few short days, they believed in the superiority of their group, and the deficiency of the out-group, to the point that they were willing to attack the others for being others.

These findings have been replicated many times in the decades since the study was first published, and almost all these studies have found that it is incredibly easy to create boundaries between two groups based on the flimsiest of starting conditions.

The implications of this for us all are frighteningly clear: *in any disagreement between our companies and our customers, our customers will almost certainly be considering us as part of the out-group, an enemy entity they must oppose.* As with the boys in the Robbers Cave study, it is much easier to create conflict than it is to create reconciliation after that conflict has begun. Of course, this isn't surprising. We can see the same effect taking place every day if we are brave enough to read the comments on Internet news articles.

In the heady summer days of 2004, a psychology researcher named Drew Westen took advantage of the fact that George W. Bush and John Kerry were in the middle of an incredibly contentious election race.[3] Westen recruited volunteers who identified as either strongly Democrat or strongly Republican, and watched the brain activity of both groups as he unleashed his own inner prankster (one thing about social science researchers is they are capable of being remarkably mischievous in their pursuit of novel research).

Westen's experiment was fairly simple. He had collected various quotes and facts about both candidates, which he used to paint them in a positive or negative light. The process was as follows and he showed volunteers three slides:

> **Slide 1:** A quote or anecdote about Bush or Kerry.
>
> **Slide 2:** A later quote or anecdote that seemed to directly contradict the first, in a way that made the politician look bad (perhaps making it seem they "flip-flopped" or exercised poor judgment).
>
> **Slide 3:** A plausible resolution to the dilemma created in the second part, which allowed the participant to "root for" the politician again if they were so inclined.

As a concrete example, they showed a quote from George W. Bush in 2000 that heavily praised Ken Lay (of

Enron infamy). The second slide (dated after the Enron fraud was known) said that Bush was critical of Enron and avoided any mention of Ken Lay. The third (reconciliation) slide explained that Bush felt personally betrayed by Lay and was genuinely shocked to learn about the corruption within Enron.

Similar patterns were found with John Kerry incidents, and both groups were shown the same sets of slides.

There were two interesting findings from this study. The first is that participants registered activity in the areas of the brain that are associated with feeling pain when their chosen candidate looked the worst (in the second slide). Similarly, there was activity in the areas of the brain associated with feeling pleasure when the third slide allowed them to reconcile the disparity. The flip side of this is that when it was the other candidate, they tended to feel pleasure when the embarrassing fact came up.

In contemporary America, there are few areas that create such instant in-group and out-group identification as politics, and the Westen study is a fantastic look at what's going on in our brains during the seemingly omnipresent political news cycle.

But this isn't just happening in politics. Anytime we see somebody we consider to be a part of our out-group hurt, our brain's first reaction is to celebrate. Similarly, when we see anybody in our in-group hurt, our brain's first reaction is to commiserate with them and feel pain. Think what you want here, but this is how we're all wired.

When a customer starts screaming at us, the odds are they're not thinking of us as part of their in-group. It's almost a certainty that they're viewing our company as the very definition of out-group, as the enemy. Whether they see the very human representative they're talking to as neutral or as just another cog in the corporate out-group will largely determine their level of hostility and how susceptible they are to reason.

When the Facts Don't Matter

It is a curious quirk of human nature that we work so much harder to disprove evidence we don't want to believe than we do to confirm that which we hope is true. The British economist John Kenneth Galbraith once famously said, "Faced with the choice between changing one's mind and proving that there is no need to do so, almost everyone gets busy on the proof,"[4] and decades' worth of psychology research has shown that he was exactly right.

Social psychologist Thomas Gilovich sums up the process of how we do this very nicely. As he explains, when people want to believe something, they ask themselves, "Can I believe this?" In contrast, when they don't want to believe something, the question they ask changes to, "Must I believe this?"[5]

When our customers see us as part of the enemy out-group, they need very little in order to believe the worst of us. When we do something that is legitimately wrong, and give them a good reason to be upset with us, they will not ask, "Must I believe that this person and this company are actively trying to harm me?" Instead, they will ask, "Can I believe that this person and this company are actively trying to harm me?" and the mere fact that they're currently angry will often be enough evidence for them that the answer is indeed yes.

We all know what it feels like to be righteously angry at being slighted by a company, which of course means being slighted by somebody within the company. After all, as we often remind our clients, a company has never bought anything or sold anything. In the history of business, nothing has ever been sold by a "company" to another "company." Behind every company, there are one or more people who are making decisions, and this is all the more relevant when we are thinking about dealing with dissatisfied customers. In effect, these customers have two targets for their anger: the individual representative of the company who was present or whose decision caused the customer to feel slighted, and the monolithic depersonalized "Company."

Of course, we would be negligent if we only considered one side of this story. It is not only foolish and shortsighted customers who mistakenly see us as an out-group enemy. Indeed, we are all too familiar with how the process works from the company's side as well. It's easy to get trapped in a paradigm that says dealing with customers is a competitive relationship, a win-lose scenario where we must stick together against the horde of unreasonable customers. Talk to any customer service rep, and they can spend hours regaling you with stories of impossible customers and their ridiculous complaints (such as the ones we started the book with!). When emotions are high in either group, it can be frighteningly easy to see the other not as a human being who is doing their best, but rather as the enemy personified.

Getting past these gut-level reactions is possible. It's certainly not easy, but any company that is committed to creating better experiences for their customers and for their employees can find ways to do it. The rest of this book will describe strategies and tactics you can use to help overcome these in-group and out-group classifications, to help your customers start to ask, "Can I believe that they have my best interest at heart?" rather than, "Can I believe that they're out to screw me?" As a last resort, this book will help you to identify and fire problem clients who are more trouble than they're worth.

This is most emphatically not a book that falls into the category that we sometimes refer to as "snappy answers to stupid questions." It will not be merely a list of situations where a dumb customer is wrong and how you can politely correct them.

Who Is a Difficult Customer?

Legendary direct response copywriter Gary Halbert was not known for his fondness for his clients. He would often teach seminars about the art of copywriting while wearing hats and T-shirts that said, "I hate clients." He was known to list the top 10 reasons that projects fail, where he just repeated the words "the client" 10 times.

Years ago, I was listening to a Gary Halbert seminar, where he said (and I'm paraphrasing very loosely here): the worst thing about customers is customers. It's a line that often brings mixed feelings. A business exists to serve a customer and we have a duty to care for customers and give our best effort and our best intent to make them happy. But what do you do when the customer can't be pleased? How do you handle the customer who seems insatiable, or as we'll refer to them in this book, *difficult*?

Why do some companies seem to be cursed with an endless stream of clients and customers who are never satisfied, for whom all work seems to fall below their standards, whereas others seem to attract the "good" customers?

Why does it seem like some customers are miserable and full of complaints when dealing with us, but quiet as a lamb when dealing with all their other providers? Forget "raving fans" and "company evangelists"—what is a person to do when a customer who leaves a business a 3-star review and calls them "adequate" would be a huge step up in the customer relationship and considered a success for the business in question?

Who's to blame?

Have those businesses simply attracted lousy customers, or are those businesses just lousy at what they do? Perhaps it's a little bit of each. With our combined experience of working with literally thousands of customers in just about every industry you can think of, we've seen it from both ends of the spectrum. Our clients have ranged from small town restaurants doing a million or two a year in annual sales, to commercial property developers, to chiropractors, to janitorial supply companies, to online and offline retailers, to extremely expensive B2B equipment manufacturers of things such as conveyor belts and gas compressors, to small contractors, to the pharmaceutical industry, to some of the biggest global fashion brands with billions of dollars in annual revenue. We've seen where the customer is always right and where the customer is always wrong. Our focus in this book is the difficult customer—the customer who seems insatiable and impossible to please. We're going to talk about all the areas your business could improve and how to do it, but it helps to first define the difficult customer. Let's get to it.

I AM A DIFFICULT CUSTOMER:
A STORY FROM A READER

It was 8:30 on a Thursday evening, and I'd just treated some prospects to a delicious dinner after spending the afternoon doing a final presentation to their board of directors about a fairly significant contract (substantial for them, and incredibly important for my business at the time). Everybody had finished up their post-dinner cocktails and desserts, and I handed the waiter my credit card to settle the bill. A few minutes later, the waiter caught my eye and subtly suggested that he needed my attention, so I excused myself from the table only to find out that my card had been declined. I was embarrassed, relieved that he hadn't announced it to the table, and grateful that I had another card I could pay with.

After the last prospect had said their goodnights, I immediately called the bank to see what the problem was. Of course, I was treated to their labyrinth of automated menu options. "Press 1 for us to not care, press 2 to be told to go to our website, press 3 then 4 then 9 to talk to a human, maybe!" I tried the standard trick of hitting 0 to get to a human.

After three tries, I was able to find a menu option that got me to a human (by picking the "My card was stolen" option), by which time my mood had darkened considerably. The agent on the line told me they'd put a stop on the card because the automatic monthly payments I'd set up through my bank (the same bank that issued the card) had stopped 45 days prior, and so they hadn't received a payment.

Though it embarrasses me a bit now to say, I was absolutely livid. "You have my phone number! You have my email address! I've had this bleeping card for 10 years, and you couldn't bother to use one of those two communication methods to let me know that a payment had been missed, and that you were going to freeze my card?" I, of course, was thinking about the damage that it would have done to my deal to have my prospects see me have a card declined over a relatively minor charge. I was thinking that if the waiter hadn't been a true professional, it probably would have sunk any chance I had at the contract.

I was thinking that in our age of interconnectivity, there's absolutely no excuse for companies not to reach out when it's important. Most of all, I was thinking about when I could schedule an appointment to switch banks and credit cards.

I love this story because it has examples of a fantastic customer-facing attitude (from the restaurant and especially the waiter), and of a really negligent attitude toward customers (from the bank/credit card company).

Most of all, I love it because it's a great reminder that nothing happens in isolation. Very few people start their day by saying, "I hope I can be rude to some call center employees today, then maybe I'll meet with some salespeople and string them along for a few more months to drive them nuts, stop in at my favorite retail shop and be a belligerent jerk to the 22-year-old associate working on the floor, and if I have time, I'll round it out by making frivolous complaints about the order of widgets I received last week."

Sometimes, a customer lashes out because they're stressed by something unrelated to you. Other times, they seem disproportionately angry about minor inconveniences, but they still bring up legitimate issues that are your company's fault. And yes, sometimes they are just horrible, and they should be fired as your clients. We'll show you how to do that later in the book.

Somebody Will Please Them: The Importance of Context and Expectations

I was talking recently to a client who is the president of a very high-end fashion brand about bad customer experiences, and she shared a great one with me.

She had booked a vacation from a website that prided itself on luxury vacations. She confided to me that the trip cost in excess of $100,000. That's not a typo; I haven't added an extra zero. She had paid for the utmost luxury and booked a trip that cost more than what most people make in a year. She explained how the website captured her heart and mind and she greatly anticipated a luxurious vacation just for her. She booked, gave a hefty deposit, and waited and heard nothing. And this was where the problems began. For the amount she was paying, she expected they would reach out to ensure all her expectations were being met. But she heard nothing. "Okay," she thought, "they're the professionals; maybe I don't need to worry about anything." She entered her luxury house and began to walk around. Things looked a bit worse for wear when compared to the website photos. Things were older, dated, and she immediately noticed the house had been poorly cleaned. She told me she could live with that, but it was what was in the fridge that set her off. Inside, she found a few chocolate bars (she doesn't eat chocolate), a six-pack of beer (she doesn't drink beer), and a dozen bottles of Coca-Cola (she doesn't drink soda). The cupboards had been filled with a few snacks such as potato chips (she doesn't eat chips) and cookies (as you guessed, she also doesn't eat cookies). Accompanied by all of this was a small note welcoming her, noting they had "stocked" the kitchen for her. Later on she told me, the house was also desperately short on towels.

When I asked her why this had bothered her so much, her answer was brilliantly simple, yet immensely enlightening: "For the amount that I paid to be there, they should have been more attentive."

It seems like a straightforward proposition. "Well, of course you expect to be treated better when you spend more money!" But this statement is at the heart of a huge percentage of cases of "difficult customers." It's a gap between what the customer thinks they're owed based on what they spend, and what the company thinks they owe their customers, in terms of product quality, service, expertise and demeanor of staff, attentiveness and attention to detail, and the totality of the experience.

In a previous book, Noah wrote about the *expectations gap*, specifically referring to the difference between what somebody thought they were buying when they decided to purchase (that is, what was marketed/sold to them) and what they received. In the following chapter, we'll be expanding that term to encompass the difference between what your prospect wants/needs from you and what you're prepared to give them.

Any time a client thinks in terms of "Given that I…this company should…" it's the expectations gap in action.

Later in the book, we'll talk about how to identify which customers are experiencing this gap, about whether you need to close it for everybody or for just a subset of customers, and about whether it is even worth closing. We'll talk about how you can minimize it early, how you can course-correct when you find it later in the relationship, and whether it's possible to eliminate it altogether.

For now, though, consider some of the complaints that you've had to deal with recently, and ask yourself, is it possible this complaint is because of an expectations gap—either inadvertently or advertently?

A Big Mac and French Laundry

Let's try a thought experiment. Picture yourself sitting down for dinner at the French Laundry—the famed restaurant of Chef Thomas Keller located in Yountville, California. You sit down and immediately notice the amazing scents drifting from the kitchen. You notice the fresh flowers on every table. You watch as the servers dance elegantly between the tables. You glance over at your neighbor's table and see the most exquisite plate your eyes have ever witnessed. At another table, you see a piece of chocolate cake delivered that has your mouth watering. You and your spouse are so excited. Your server arrives and introduces herself. She seems pleasant and you both order your meals. The appetizers and wine are out of this world. The anticipation for the main course is building; after all, you made your reservation three months ago.

Finally, we want you to imagine that throughout the meal, you begin to notice a hint of condescension from your waiter. It's nothing you could put your finger on, but something that rubbed you the wrong way. Imagine telling your spouse about that feeling and hearing that they felt the same way. "I didn't want to say anything, but yes…I definitely noticed it!"

Now, imagine yourself at a McDonald's for a quick lunch-stop between meetings. Though it's recently renovated, the decor is worlds apart from your experience at Thomas Keller's flagship restaurant. You only have about 20 minutes until you need to be on the road, and truth be told, you've been craving a Big Mac for quite some time.

Three minutes go by.

Four.

Five.

You're looking at your phone, watching others take their orders, and doing the math to figure out how quickly you'll have to finish this meal before you need to leave. Finally, after eight minutes, your order is up, and you enjoy a somewhat rushed lunch. You know the time it took them to get your food to you was about three times as long as they typically strive for, and truth be told, the rush caused you to not really enjoy the meal at all.

Now, in which of these scenarios would you be more likely to lodge a complaint?

Which of them would cause you to tell a friend about your bad experience?

Which of them would still bother you a week later?

If you're anything like me, and the hundreds of people I've put this scenario to, the answer is screamingly obvious: the French Laundry experience would be worse, by a very wide margin. "Given how much I paid for the French Laundry experience; given their reputation, and what I was looking forward to; given how much others had raved about it, I would have expected to be made to feel more welcome."

Very few people have any expectations at all when going to McDonald's. Everybody has expectations when going to the French Laundry. And the higher the expectations are, the easier it is to dash them. This gives us a simple prescription to eliminate the expectations gap altogether: tell all your clients that you've decided to stop trying, that you're going to reduce your prices to bargain-basement levels, and that they can stick around with you if they wish. Guaranteed, there'll be no more dissatisfied customers amongst the ones who stay!

Okay, maybe not.

For those who would prefer to remain profitable, who don't want to compete solely on price, and who think it's great that their customers have expectations that need to be lived up to, the rest of this book is for you.

A Simple Tool to Please the Difficult: The Hierarchy of Horrors

Let's shift gears and talk about a few of the tools you can use to understand why you might be dealing with unhappy customers and the things your business can do internally to reduce the number of problems and challenges you have when it comes to serving your customers.

When I first met Shawn, he introduced me to a fantastic tool I've gone on to use in organizations doing billions of dollars in annual sales. The reason we like to re-use this process is because it's drop-dead simple and incredibly powerful when used properly. Shawn told me about a great book by one of the founding officers of FedEx, Michael Basch, titled *Customer Culture: How FedEx and Other Great Companies Put the Customer First Every Day.* In the book, Basch introduced what he said was one of the key components for FedEx's success in the early days. It was a simple process they called the *hierarchy of horrors.*[6]

Here's what they did. FedEx got all their executives together in a room and they spent a couple of hours coming up with the eight worst things they could do to upset their customers. The list included things such as damaging a customer's package, losing a package, missing a scheduled delivery or pick-up, delivering goods to the wrong house, delivering late or not at all, and so on. Each of the identified problem areas was measured for about a month using a simple checklist. Each time a mistake was made, they checked a box. As soon as another mistake was made, they checked another box, and at the end of

30 days, they tallied everything up to see which mistake they were making most often. Remember, these were the top causes of customer unhappiness. They ranked the horrific mistakes from bad, to worse, to the worst. The area they were messing up the most was the area to start on first. As you can see, this gave them a great opportunity to systematically look at all the ways they were upsetting their customers, and it gave them a simple, easy-to-follow roadmap of the areas they needed to improve on.

What they discovered was that late packages caused the most grief for customers, so that's where they focused first. They held everyone accountable and worked to fix this one single area of their business during the next 30 days. When they had significantly reduced the number of times they were delivering packages late, they moved on to the next area.

We're going to be talking about all kinds of unhappy and seemingly difficult customers in this book, but that doesn't mean it's always the customer's fault. FedEx realized very early on that most of their unpleasant customer interactions were things totally within their control to improve, fix, or even eliminate. There are reasons FedEx became FedEx, and this is one of them. Let's review a simple process that you can use within your company starting today.

How to Define Your Hierarchy of Horrors

Step One: List Your Company's Biggest Mistakes

Get honest here. Ask yourself, what are the things my company does that create unpleasant feelings for its customers? What are the worst things it does to make a customer unhappy? Don't be shy here. Remember, FedEx was brutally honest with itself! Their whole positioning in the marketplace was about fast, on-time, reliable delivery; meeting and closing the expectations gap is the magic bullet, it is the Philosopher's Stone, it is the Royal Road to customer happiness.

Step Two: Measure for 30 Days

Find a way to measure all the times you make these mistakes during a 30-day period. You can use tools as simple as an Excel file or even a checklist in most businesses. Just check each time the mistake is made. Naturally, you'll be fixing the mistakes and dealing with unhappy customers as you go, but for now, we just want to gauge the 8–10 things you're messing up the most and seeing which is happening most often.

Here's another important point to keep in mind: not all of these mistakes will be geared toward customer grievances. For example, FedEx was looking primarily at their internal screw-ups that affected the customer experience and created disgruntled customers. However, all of these screw-ups also had a direct impact on the profitability of the company and their ability to thrive in the future. They wanted to know how often delivery trucks were late, or how often packages were mishandled. They realized that each time a mistake was made, it cost the company a lot more than a single complaint. Remember, one unhappy customer can cause companies millions in lost future revenues.

Step Three: Order Your Results

After you've measured for at least 30 days, prioritize the list so the horrors are ordered from bad to worst.

Considering that you're talking about the "horrors"—the worst possible mistakes being made with your customers—they're all going to feel like pretty big issues. It might be a bit shocking, and if you're not honest, this process will never be as powerful as it could be, but sit down with your team and take a good terrifying look at the horrors. If you can't come to an agreement on how to prioritize, look at which mistake was made most often or simply pick one and start. They're all horrors and they're all scary! Working on one of them will make an improvement. One large manufacturing client told the story of how a single mistake cost tens of thousands of dollars each time it was made. The hierarchy of horrors allowed his company to identify the mistake and to work on improving that area to save literally millions each year and avoid dealing with plenty of difficult customers.

Step Four: Get Started!

Now that you've got a systematic roadmap for all the ways you're upsetting your customers, you've just got to get started. Pick one single area and work on improving your result. The goal here is to focus on small improvements. If you made the mistake 12 times through the course of 30 days, aim to make it only eight times in the following month, and maybe three times after that. Keep working at it until you virtually eliminate the horror, and then move on to the next horror.

You need to ensure there's accountability for the reduction of the horrors. If one department was making a mistake twice each day, see if it can quickly reduce that number. Also, you should create and accept feedback from those charged with reducing the horrors. Sometimes your employees or parts of your team might have suggestions and answers that will drastically reduce the horrors. So the question is: do you have a way for members of your team to offer their feedback in a way it can be considered and acted upon?

This is such a simple model, yet it can have such a dramatic impact on any organization. Most companies wonder why they're dealing with so many customer service related issues, and it's really quite simple. Customers don't leave the theater smiling and wishing for more—they often leave scared out of their wits. Fix the horrors and you'll have happy customers. It's really that simple.

Case Study: Hierarchy of Horrors in Action

I was working with a company that wanted to get serious about identifying their biggest problem issues and working to correct them. They had a number of locations across the country, and every day their call center received hundreds of calls from prospective clients, existing clients, and sometimes dissatisfied clients.

What we did with this company was categorize every single complaint that came in. As new issues reared, we created new categories. Then, we built a simple dashboard that could be seen by everybody in the company. It showed, for each location, the number of clients who had been served during the past week, and the number of issues that had come in. Everybody in the company could see exactly how each location was doing in terms of percentage of issues, and then drill through to find out what types of issues were most prevalent.

This had a number of incredibly powerful effects very quickly.

First and foremost, it brought to light that some locations were just plain better at creating experiences for customers that didn't result in any issues down the road.

Second, it made it screamingly obvious what issues were most common at any point in time, ensuring that no issues were hiding from management.

Third, it created quite the incentive for every location to actively look for ways to reduce these issues—nobody wanted to explain why, for the fourth week in a row, they still had the highest rates of the most damaging incidents.

Put Your Customer Hat On

You picked this book up for a reason, but the obvious and most stunning thing staring us all in the face is that we're all customers! You and I are both customers of a variety of businesses nearly every day of our lives. One of the most powerful business lessons I ever learned about sales and marketing is that customers don't wake up every day asking themselves how they can give you more money. Just like you and I are customers, your customers wake up every day with the same things going on in their lives that we have going on. There might be family problems, financial issues, illness in the family, work and job stress—you get the idea! Sometimes, we take off our customer hat because we're wearing the business owner/executive hat. We often forget that we're dealing with people, just like you and me. But how customers are treated in your business is likely directly related to how you think about them. Are customers a gift who put food on your table and feed your family? Are they the gift that keeps you employed at your organization? Or do you see them as a giant pain in the butt?

How do you really feel about customers? Consider the following statements and ask yourself if they are true or false.

1. My customers expect way too much.

2. My customers are cheap and unwilling to spend for better service.

3. My customers are too demanding.

4. Even though the saying goes "the customer is always right," my customers are almost always wrong.

5. Our customers aren't very loyal.

6. Our better customers deserve better service than customers who don't spend as much money.

7. Customers complain about everything! Even the small stuff.

Regardless of how you answered, think about them now in the frame that I mentioned before sharing the quiz. More importantly, put yourself in the customer's shoes. Put your customer hat on for a minute and let's give the customer the benefit of the doubt.

1. My customers expect way too much. Do your customers really expect too much, or do they expect the service they paid for? More importantly, have you created an expectations gap by overpromising the customer? Many customer complaints and difficult customers are created by the simple fact they don't get what was actually promised to them. The majority of this book has been about helping you deal with that.

2. My customers are cheap and unwilling to spend for better service. Do you know if that's true? I've heard this from many businesses in the past, but almost none of them have done anything to show me or prove the claim. Have you tried to create new offerings and products that can provide better and faster service? Here's an example: are you an Amazon Prime customer? If you are, I rest my case. Amazon created an entire business, and billions of dollars in subscription revenue, by selling the right for faster and better service.

3. My customers are too demanding. Are you too demanding when it comes to getting what you paid for? If you don't feel like you got what you paid for, do you sometimes become difficult, disagreeable, and dissatisfied?

4. Even though the saying goes "the customer is always right," my customers are almost always wrong. I've heard businesses say this. How would you feel as a customer if the businesses you buy from were saying this about you? (They might be right now!)

5. Our customers aren't very loyal. As I noted in my other books, customer loyalty is never owed. Customer loyalty has to be earned through day-in-and-day-out marketing. I'm sure you've fallen out of habit of doing business with those you once frequented. You've most likely bought from competitors even though you were "loyal" to one specific business. Do you expect loyalty from your customers, or are you earning it?

6. Our better customers deserve better service than customers who don't spend as much money. All people who decide to open their wallets should get the same level of service. Imagine yourself as a customer and receiving really poor service just because it was your first time doing business with someone. You wouldn't like that at all and you certainly don't deserve that. It's like being told by the hostess, "Sorry, there are absolutely no tables," but then seeing a concession made for someone the hostess personally knows. It stings.

7. Customers complain about everything! Even the small stuff. Again, put your customer hat on for a minute. You likely complain about everything when there's a problem, and you likely complain about the small stuff when there's even a small problem (for example, the server took too long to bring our drinks; the store associate didn't say hello; the manufacturing rep didn't return my email as promised). But most loyal customers are willing to brush off the odd mistake as an anomaly. Here's what I mean: think about your favorite restaurant, the one that you and your spouse love to visit every week. You're loyal, and if they make an odd mistake, you're not going to stop going there. In fact, the odd mistake is nothing more than just a blip because consistency trumps all. Remember, being consistently good is better than being great once in a while.

What we'll see in this book is that the assumptions we have about our customers directly affect the way we treat them and the way they in turn behave. More often than not, poor customer service is a result of an *expectations gap* between the customer and the company. By applying the tools of this book to your training and everyday practice, you'll learn how to see your customers in the most flattering light, teach them what they can reasonably expect of you, and sow the seeds for much smoother interactions.

Chapter 2

Managing Expectations: What They Want vs. What You Deliver

Don't Trust the Juice

Take a second to answer a very easy question: when it comes to customer service, and your efforts to go above and beyond for your customers, how would you rate yourself on a scale from 1 to 10?

We'll make our guess as to your answer in a couple of pages, and you can see how close we get. In the meantime, consider this story.

It was just above 10 degrees in Pittsburgh on January 6, 1996, when a 270 lb. man standing 5'6" walked into a bank in Brighton Heights, smiled directly in the face of the security camera, and then proceeded to rob the bank. Later in the day and just 12 miles away, he robbed another bank in Swissvale, with a similar lack of concern about being spotted by the security cameras. Smile, wave, nod. Rob the bank.

It took a couple of months, but eventually the police got a copy of the surveillance tapes and had them broadcast on the nightly news, and within the hour, they were knocking on the door of McArthur Wheeler. His only comment? "But I wore the juice!"

Some of Wheeler's friends had told him that much like lemon juice could be used as invisible ink in elementary school science class, it could also be used to make you invisible to cameras. Not being the trusting sort, Wheeler applied lemon juice to his face and then snapped a selfie with his trusty Polaroid camera, and was delighted when he didn't see himself in it.

Maybe it was the sting of the lemon juice in his eyes (which he later complained made it almost impossible for him to see) that caused him to aim the camera poorly, or maybe he just had some faulty film—either way, he was convinced that he could become invisible to cameras. He was so convinced, in fact, that he confidently went on to rob two banks, and was genuinely shocked to see his own face on the security footage when the police showed it to him.

The story was repeated in the 1996 edition of the *World Almanac* as one of the features under the heading of "World's Dumbest Criminals," where it caught the eye of Cornell professor David Dunning.[1] Dunning and his graduate student Justin Kruger were intrigued by the story and recognized a seemingly universal trend of those who are least skilled or knowledgeable being most confident in their abilities and knowledge. They conducted a series of studies showing what would later be dubbed the Dunning-Kruger effect. The effect, in short, shows that most people, regardless of how they perform on most tasks, rate themselves at about 7/10 on that task.

McArthur Wheeler is often used as the poster child for the Dunning-Kruger effect, but we think he gets a bad rap in this respect. He was skeptical of his friends' claims about the lemon juice. He knew they might be messing with him, so he ran an experiment with his Polaroid by taking a selfie, and enacted a strategy based on his results. If you're reading this book, chances are you've been in boardrooms where companies made significant investment decisions based on hunches, hearsay, and the highest paid person's opinion without conducting even a "lemon-faced selfie" experiment. The sad truth here is this: when it comes to accurately judging our skills, performance, and chances of success, we're often a lot more like McArthur Wheeler than we are comfortable admitting. Is your company trusting the juice? And if you're curious, he never saw himself in the photo which gave him the confidence to move forward. He believed his friends were indeed telling the truth. Police suspect he had too much lemon juice in his eyes, or maybe he pointed the camera the wrong way—they never really figured that part of the story out.

The Lake Wobegon Effect:
Are You as Good as You Think You Are?

In central Minnesota, near Stearns County, up around Holdingford, not far from St. Rosa, Albany, and Freeport, northwest of St. Cloud, there's a little town that time forgot and the decades cannot improve. It's a place where all the women are strong, all the men are good-looking, and all the children are above average.

Fans of Garrison Keillor will immediately recognize the hallmarks of Lake Wobegon, whereas almost everybody else will be wondering what this fictional town has to do with a book on pleasing the difficult customer.

The Lake Wobegon effect (or illusory superiority) is a term that psychologists use to describe a near universal tendency for people to overrate their ability compared to "average" in a huge variety of tasks.

In one survey, 93 percent of drivers said they're in the top 50 percent when it comes to skill, and 88 percent said they were in the top half when it came to safety.[2] Of professors surveyed, 68 percent think they're in the top 25 percent, and more than 90 percent said they were above average.[3] Of more than one million respondents surveyed, 25 percent put themselves in the top 1 percent of the population when it comes to getting along with others.[4] In another study, 38 percent of people said they were better drivers *while texting* than the average driver who was concentrating on the road.[5]

At the start of this chapter, we asked you to write down the score you gave yourself when it came to all things customer service. Based on the Dunning-Kruger effect, and the wider implications of the Lake Wobegon effect, we're betting it was 7. Whatever it was, do you want to revise your answer? Lake Wobegon and the hilarity of one the world's dumbest criminals offer us the perfect illustration of one of the reasons companies deal with more customer unhappiness than they would like: the expectations gap.

The Expectations Gap, Revisited

In its simplest form, the expectations gap can be illustrated with the following exchange:

> **Customer:** "You know, with how much I've spent, and how long I've been a client, I'd expect they would try a little harder, but no such luck!"

> **Company:** "You know, considering the high quality product we offer, the service we back it up with, and the low price we ask, you'd think they'd cut us a little slack, but no such luck!"

The expectations gap is the term for the difference between what a customer was sold and what they get in return. This gap can be created intentionally through overzealous sales and marketing from the company or inadvertently through fantastic word of mouth. "You absolutely must try this restaurant—it was the best meal that I have ever had in my 70 years of traveling this planet, and I guarantee that absolutely everything you taste will put you in a state of bliss unrivalled by even the most powerful drug!"

Companies have to maintain a careful balance between making their products and services sound as appealing as possible and preparing new customers for the inevitable less-than-perfect experiences they may come across. Failure to manage the expectations gap is one of the most common reasons we lose customers early or create feelings of resentment and unhappiness within our customers. The world of sales and marketing has improved at a rate far outpacing the improvement of the simple delivery of products and services or customer service. We've gotten too good at writing copy, creating persuasive advertising, driving traffic, and converting sales. The expectations gap continues to grow in many industries.

When we work with companies to identify the sources of the expectations gap, one of the first exercises we do is to ask the same questions to four groups of people: senior executives, frontline staff, happy customers, and difficult customers.

The two questions we ask them are "From a customer point of view, tell me what the best thing about [insert any company name] is, and what the worst thing is."

	Senior Executive	Frontline Staff	Happy Customer	Difficult Customer
Best thing about company	"We bend over backwards for our customers. We go out of our way to give them the best experience, every time."	[generally positive comment]	[generally positive]	"They haven't run out of stock, yet."
Worst thing about company	"There are a couple of minor issues that we're working on; they should be fixed by next quarter."	"We really have no autonomy to help customers; we have to tell them how much we value them, but aren't given the authority or tools to actually resolve their complaints beyond giving them a discount when they complain too much."	[mildly negative]	"I've had the same issues with them for two years. The few times I've complained I've been brushed off, and nothing has really changed."

Without fail, there is a huge difference in how the different respondents see the company, and their beliefs about whether it's the company or the customer at fault in any given disagreement. Hard as it is for most companies to recognize, this is really good news because it means there is hope for reconciling the way the customers view the company with the dreams the senior executives have for it.

The Bizarro Business World of Customer Happiness

In April of 1960, DC Comics, the publisher of the popular Superman comics, threw its readers for a loop. They introduced Bizarro World where everything was the opposite of the way it should be. In the Bizarro World of "htraE" ("Earth" spelled backward), society is ruled by the Bizarro Code which states, "Us do opposite of all Earthly things! Us hate beauty! Us love ugliness! Is big crime to make anything perfect on Bizarro World!"[6] In one episode, for example, a salesman is doing a brisk trade selling Bizarro bonds: "Guaranteed to lose money for you." Later, the mayor appoints Bizarro No. 1 to investigate a crime, "Because you are stupider than the entire Bizarro police force put together." This is intended and taken as a great compliment.

Originally a normal planet, htraE is now cube-shaped. This is due to the intervention of Superman, who after being convicted of doing something perfect on htraE, which would normally be a capital offense, pointed out that the planet was shaped like a normal spheroid and agreed to cube it if his sentence were commuted.

We've often found that one of the easiest ways to understand the expectations gap is to flip the problem of problem customers on its head by creating our own Bizarro World view of your own company. Instead of trying to figure out how to please the difficult, let's imagine that the primary goal of our company is to have as many unhappy customers as we can. Seriously. Let's go and get a pile of new customers guaranteed to be grumpy and generally difficult. We can attract them so they're unhappy from day one, or we can enrage our existing customers, or we can combine both strategies for an ultra-effective campaign to generate the maximum amount of hate. Sounds like fun, right? Bear with us and enjoy this Business Bizarro World.

Attracting the Difficult Customers

With our new goal of generating as many dissatisfied customers as we can, we start in the same place many companies start: by trying to figure out how to get more new customers in the door! Sure, the "experts" tell us that it's 10 times more effective to turn an existing happy customer into a difficult customer, but we'd rather go out and find a whole new group of voices to yell at us. That seems like a far worthier endeavor.

Where to start?

Focus Only on Price

The best way to start our attraction of the difficult customer is to make the sole content of our messaging and branding revolve around having the lowest prices or having lots of sales. With luck, we'll be able to coordinate a Groupon special to bring in a bus-load of new, price-sensitive customers.

At the same time, we want to use targeted advertising and direct marketing to find our competitors' customers, and promise them that we can save them 0.5 percent off the price they're paying with their current suppliers. By doing this, we'll ensure that we're getting customers who are willing to jump ship—with a total absence of any "customer loyalty"—for the tiniest of price decreases, which means they place no value on service, experience, or any factor other than the price per unit.

But remember, this is about bringing in difficult customers, not just price-conscious customers. How can we enrage these new customers if we know they don't put any real value on service or their overall experience? Surely, it won't be enough to just have bad service; they'll likely expect that, given that they're willing to come to us on price alone.

In order to generate hate from this group, we're going to have to show them what they were taking for granted with their previous suppliers. We'll make late deliveries, forget to include stock in the orders, deliver the lowest quality, and make it hard to order and re-order—the whole shebang of lousy.

Lead From Gold: Making Existing Customers Difficult

Well, we've learned that the expectations gap is a pretty big factor in creating customer dissatisfaction, so it only makes sense in Bizarro World to find ways to maximize that gap. Here are a few areas we can create maximum discrepancy between our customers' expectations of us and our expectations of them.

Price vs. Attentiveness

The most obvious place to start is to place ourselves at a premium price in our market space, with a price of at least 120–150 percent higher than our nearest competitor. Next (and this is very important), we'll spend time training our staff how to ignore our customers. If we're in retail, we'll train our salespeople to take personal calls, talk to each other, rush past customers on their way to the stock room without stopping, and generally avoid eye contact. We know that this is unnatural for them, but we assure them that it's our goal to make people uncomfortable and angry, so we need to make them approach us and make it as awkward as possible for them to get any attention. What else can we do in Bizarro World?

Slogans vs. Service (a.k.a. What's Written on the Walls vs. What's Said in the Halls)

Our next tactic is also quite simple. We'll invest heavily in creating incredibly vague mission statements ("The customer is #1! We put quality first! We want to be world leaders in service!"), then invest further to advertise these slogans, feature them prominently on our website, post them in our stores, and instruct our staff to repeat them to all of our clients. At the same time, we'll brainstorm with our staff on ways we can demonstrate exactly the opposite, or to interpret the slogans in ironic ways.

> **Director:** "Okay, point one, we said that our primary objective is to create unforgettable experiences for our clients. How can we dash that expectation?"

> **Store Manager:** "Well, what if we put into place an automated phone system that was impossible to navigate, changed every two months, and only had one option that actually connected our clients to a human being?"

> **Sales Associate 1:** "Ooh, I like that idea! And what if half of the other options were just telling our clients that we have a website, indicating to them that we think they might be time travelers from 1996 and not expect a major player such as ourselves to have an Internet presence!"

> **Director:** "That's great stuff, guys! Let's also make sure the system automatically hangs up on

them if they take too long to respond. Good. Now let's think about our outbound efforts. What if we have our salespeople call them without doing any preparatory work, show up to presentations with pitch decks that were obviously cut and pasted from previous clients, and not let them get a word in edgewise until we finish spewing out our pre-canned sales presentations at them?"

Website vs. On-Site

Now that we've set our prices high, trained our staff to be inattentive, and found creative ways to show our customers how little we think of them (while at the same time spending time and money telling them how important they are), let's go to work on the marketing side. Because our goal is to bring in as many new customers as we can and then disappoint them in short order, we'll want to create a wildly misleading picture of what doing business with us will look like. This is a particularly good place for destination-focused companies to shine—those in the hospitality and travel industry have an incredible opportunity to use pictures of their locations that are a few years out of date, showing an immediate post-renovation state vs. the current shoddy appearance. We can throw in pictures of smiling groups of models we've hired, and not the actual pictures of harried customers yelling fruitlessly at our location managers.

Inconsistency in Service Levels
(the Anti-McDonald's)

One of the most counterintuitive findings in the customer service world is that universally poor service isn't necessarily a death knell for a company. Where most companies get into trouble is when they have typically average or even good service, interspersed with the occasional head-scratchingly bad service.

This makes sense when we take the time to think about it, of course. With universally bad service, customers will either leave or get used to it and build it into their expectations. The expectations gap for companies with universally bad service is, ironically, extremely low. These universally poor service companies can even score the occasional win by providing merely subpar instead of awful service. People will leave feeling better about the company than if they'd received merely great instead of excellent service from a company they expected the best from.

With that in mind, and with our goal of enraging as many customers as possible, we need to add one last element to our Bizarro World strategy: occasionally superb service.

Randomly, throughout the year, we should ensure that we treat our clients like royalty and show them the white glove treatment before cruelly ripping it away in our next interaction with them.

Meanwhile, Back on Earth...

Okay, that was fun, but let's get back to reality. Of course, it's never going to be our goal to enrage as many customers as possible. We want to do the opposite, so let's make sure that we learn the lessons of the Bizarro World companies, and put sane practices and policies into place in our own companies.

The 50,000-foot view rule is simple and so bland as to be a cliché: act with integrity.

Put simply, do what you say that you're going to do. Be hyper-attentive to the implicit and explicit messages that you're sending to your prospective and existing customers, and ensure that your actions match those messages.

Note that we're not recommending "Make every experience unforgettable!" or even "Find ways to wow your customers." There is a place for that, in some companies at some times, but it must be preceded by consistently acting with integrity.

You can be a world-class business while offering almost no customer interaction, low-quality products, and the bare minimum customer "experience," as long as your customers are under no illusion about what to expect when they walk in your doors or hand their credit cards to you.

On the flip side, you can have the best product, incredible customer service, and create truly amazing experiences, but if even 10 percent of the time one of these areas slip, then you're likely to alienate a huge chunk of your audience. We've come to realize that inconsistency is the real killer, and this is even truer when the frequency of customer interactions is high.

The Importance of Knowing Your Customer

There's a fun, simple workshop exercise that has sort of given us "cult-like status" with many of the clients we work with. It's such a simple exercise, but one we're often asked to repeat when hired to work with a client's staff at all levels, from the executive team, to sales, marketing, and all customer-facing employees. I've written about this in many locations, but it's worth repeating here because it's so darn important when it comes to fostering loyalty and maximizing profits with your best customers, and creating those unpleasant feelings with others. We call it The Walter White Workshop. I've received calls from companies asking us to literally just come and do the "Walter White" with their sales and marketing teams.

We use this exercise to illustrate a few very important points. Many companies and their employees are communicating with, marketing to, or attempting to sell and service to customers they don't really know or truly understand. It's one thing not to truly understand the customer you're trying to attract, but the core lesson of this exercise becomes even more powerful when you realize you also don't know them enough to understand what will upset them.

Now you're probably wondering, why would companies be interested in having us do an exercise named after one of the main characters from the popular television show *Breaking Bad*, and how does this big exercise work?

Here's how it works. There are two simple steps. First, we ask everyone in the room to flip over a piece of paper and spend the next 3–5 minutes writing down everything they know about one of their favorite TV characters. The first time we did this exercise was at the Evergreen Summit, an annual event that I put on every year; you should join us (see TheEvergreenSummit.com). Heads were down and people in the room were furiously writing detailed narratives and descriptions of their favorite TV characters. When I had them stop writing to tell me about the characters, at least half a dozen people in the room chose Walter White. They were able to tell the most detailed, vivid descriptions of Walter, from what type of car he drove, to where he worked, where he lived, how many children he had, what he was and wasn't interested in, how he spent his free time, and so on. The story repeated itself throughout the room where people described in such illustrative detail these fictional characters that only entered their lives once a week. That's step one of the Walter White Exercise.

Now we move on to step two where I ask them to flip over another sheet of paper, and then I give them one simple task: spend another 3–5 minutes writing as much as you can about your ideal customer.

What do you think happens?

Blank stares. Blank faces. No feverish writing sessions. The very marketers who draft copy and create advertisements for attracting these very people struggle to write anything about them. The same salespeople who talk to these customers on a daily basis have a hard time putting down on paper what they know about their customers.

When we first did this at the inaugural Evergreen Summit, within a few seconds, one of the guests looked up and shouted out, "Okay Noah, we get the point!" There was laughter throughout the room, but it was instantly apparent it was far more difficult to describe our current and prospective clients than it was to describe a fictional TV character. Think about that. This is a big deal. The exercise is fun, but it's incredibly illustrative. Now, of course, most of us have many different customers and types of customers. There isn't a one-size-fits-all description. However, most companies also think they understand their customers well enough to understand their buying motives and what makes them tick, but if you pressed them on this, as I did, you'd learn that most only understand them on a surface level. That's not enough. That's why we have an expectations gap. That's exactly why some customers can't be pleased, and why some companies struggle and seem to continuously attract the worst, most disgruntled customers on the planet. Could it be that we simply don't understand our customers as well as we should?

Try the Walter White Exercise in all areas of your company and you'll quickly recognize just another area where you're likely inadvertently creating a huge expectations gap.

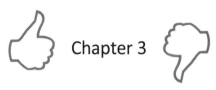 Chapter 3

Buying vs. Selling:
Creating Greater Alignment

The Death of the Trusted Advisor

As buyers, it can sometimes be hard to remember the experience of purchasing high-ticket items in the pre-Internet age. The scarcity of information available about almost anything we wanted to purchase was staggering, leading to quite a large power gap between buyers and salespeople. Low-performing salespeople hate the change that's occurred during the past 20 years in this regard. They long for the days when reading the manufacturer's product sheet was enough to allow them to generate substantial commissions with minimal effort. We still have many clients with salespeople to this day insisting they need more product sheets, catalogs, and information. Sometimes that's true; more often than not, it's not.

I bring this up not to rehash every sales book since 2001 that caused me to gasp and faint because they expelled so much hot air about how the Internet turned the world upside down and how we need to be better than ever to sell to newly savvy customers; instead, I want to point out that this deluge of information about any and all products has, in some ways, been just as negatively impactful on our customers.

In the bad old days, especially for high-ticket items, customers had little choice but to find a salesperson they liked and were prepared to trust and take them at their word that whatever was being sold was top of the line. Once they'd made a purchasing decision, they utilized the asset and went on with their lives. Some got better deals than others, and some unlucky few were sold on the wonders of Betamax over VHS, or on Yugos instead of Hondas, but all in all, the system worked.

Then, almost overnight, the world went topsy-turvy. Customers were suddenly able to ask deeply insightful and penetrating questions about your product lines, sometimes seeming to know more about what you sold than you did. Pricing information was no longer something you could wait until the latter stages of the sale because customers already knew your price, your competitor's price, and everybody's price. Most of them had a better sense of what your competitors were offering, given that it was now easier than ever to compare quotes from vendors around the world. No matter where you were, you were suddenly in competition with an entire planet, not just a neighborhood.

Customers, seeing their salespeople flounder and choke when trying to answer questions simple enough to be answered with their 10 minutes of research, began to doubt the ability (and/or motivation) of their salespeople to truly act in their best interest. I remember my last car buying experience, where I knew more about the car's new features than the sales rep knew about the car he was selling. I found myself teaching him! Even post-purchase, customers were able to compare what they had bought to what was on offer from others, masochistically asking themselves if they made the right choice.

If the salespeople could no longer answer even the simplest of probing questions, then *why should the customers trust them to be able to help with more abstract questions?*

Therein lies one of the least discussed, but most impactful consequences of the information age on the buying and selling processes. Customers have begun to commoditize every offer, treating salespeople as order takers and purveyors of information about how minor details compare, and they have lost the capacity to trust their salespeople to help guide them to the wisest purchases.

Salespeople became trained by the majority of their customers to be order takers, and lost the ability to garner the trust and rapport with their client base for anything beyond order taking. From there, the posture of sales organizations shifted to the new-world selling solution of the "trusted advisor."

A Revolutionary Way to Think About Sales That Might Melt Your Brain

If you read enough sales books, you'll start to notice a pattern very quickly. They typically all start with some variation of the following.

Way back in the good old days, selling was a simple matter. You could just wander around with a big wooden club, hit your prospects over the head with it, and rifle through their wallets while they were unconscious.

But somewhere along the way, customers started wearing helmets, and our old methods stopped working. To sell to today's modern, sophisticated clients, you need to use our specialized selling method, the likes of which you've never seen before. And if you don't, your children will starve and your spouse will leave.

Step 1: Try to think about your prospects as real human beings, instead of just wallets.

Step 2: Maybe ask them a question or two before you launch into your pitch and tell them how wonderful you are.

Step 3: If they object to anything, repeat your pitch louder. Their objections are just getting you closer to a yes!

Step 4: Profit.

I've always found these kinds of introductions to be quite insulting. I can't imagine the target audience the authors have in mind while writing them, but they bear no resemblance to the sales professionals that I work with on a daily basis.

I'm not going to tell you that I'm here to revolutionize the way you look at selling. You wouldn't still be in business if you were as inept as the typical sales author thinks you are. What I will do in this chapter is ask you to broaden your thinking and expand your definitions of service, sales, and of what's happening in your buyer's mind.

By doing so, you'll find opportunities to reduce frictions that would otherwise lead to dissatisfied customers, and hopefully find some new ways to bring even more value to your clients and prospects.

What Is the Salesperson's Most Important Job?

Even though the room was air conditioned, I could feel the sweat trickling down my neck as I stood in front of a group of 30 salespeople I'd been hired to give a keynote address to. Although it wasn't my first time speaking in front of people, it was the first time I was starting a talk with this exercise, and I was terrified that it would backfire on me.

But it was too late to back out now. I'd been introduced, received the polite applause that everybody gives to a speaker they've never heard, and it was time to start.

"We're nearing the end of the quarter, and you're probably wondering why we're all together now instead of letting you sell, right?" I asked. They laughed a little, but

I could see it was a question that most of the people in the room were indeed asking themselves.

"Before we get started, I have a question for you. Just shout out the answer. What is your most important job, as salespeople?"

Before I tell you their answer, and my response, I'll ask you now: what is the most important job of a salesperson and of a sales team?

This group was not shy. Their answers came back quickly:

"To sell!" (A few of them followed this up with comments impugning my intelligence for asking such a simple question.)

"To meet our quota!"

"To make the company money!"

"To fill the pipeline with real deals!"

I could relax—the gambit had worked, they'd answered as I'd expected, and the rest of the keynote went off without a hitch. I've refined the content quite a bit since then, but the heart of my message to that group remains the same, which is what this chapter is all about.

The Salesperson's Most Important Job

I've run this little experiment hundreds of times since then in keynotes, in webinars, in one-on-one conversations with salespeople, sales managers, presidents, CEOs, hiring managers, and everybody else whose job brings them close to sales within their companies, and I almost always get the same answers as that first group gave me.

Savvy reader that you are, I'm sure you recognized the "trick" of the question: the salesperson's most important job isn't to sell, but to *help* both prospects and clients alike to *buy*. *Help to buy*.

If you think the difference is one of semantics, you're not alone. It seems like such a slight difference that it's not even worth mentioning, but I am going to mention it. Indeed, I'm going to spend the rest of this chapter mentioning it and continue to mention it throughout the book. This distinction is the difference between companies who struggle to deal with difficult customers and those who get hand-written thank you notes from their client base. It's the difference between being mediocre and being great.

When I run this exercise with most people and groups, the first response is almost always to wave away the difference, to say, "They're two sides of the same coin; I was right," or to say, "That's a hippy-dippy way of looking at it. Salespeople sell; it's right there in the name. There's no dressing it up."

If your first thought was along those lines, I'm asking you to keep an open mind as you read this chapter. If I do my job, you'll finish the chapter with a new perspective on sales and selling, and most importantly with a new appreciation for what your prospects and customers are looking for.

And if I don't, well, at least you'll have a fun party trick next time you're surrounded by salespeople.

The Difference Between Buying and Being Sold

One of the oldest truisms in the sales world is that everybody likes buying and nobody likes being sold. We all know this, and so it's especially telling when it's crunch time, sales professionals the world around default to language that puts the onus on them to "make sales" rather than to "help their prospects and customers buy."

Salespeople are taught that to "close the deal," they first need to "control the sale," instead of being told that they can best serve their clients and prospects by being professional enough to know the right set of questions to ask in order to help the prospect understand their options and make the best choice.

Sales managers desperately push their people to "close out the quarter" in any way possible, whether it means offering discounts or relentlessly hounding everybody in the latter stages of the funnel.

The language we use matters—it shapes the way we think and the way others think about us. Minor differences in how we phrase things (to others and to ourselves) have incredible impact. If you don't believe me, the next time you mean to ask your spouse, "What's the matter?" see what response you get if you substitute it with "What's wrong with you?" instead.

The truth of business is not "Nothing happens until something gets sold." The reality is that "Nothing happens until somebody buys." Buying is a choice that your customers make each with their own set of criteria. Selling is what we do to facilitate that choice for our prospects and clients.

Enough with the setup; let's dive in and look at the differences between buying and being sold, talk about what this has to do with dealing with customers, and turning demanding, dissatisfied, and disagreeable customers into your best customers. Trust us, it's important.

The Four Stages of Customer Readiness

Broadly speaking, all your prospects and clients are spread out between four stages of readiness to buy, each of which requires a very different approach to marketing and selling. Trying to sell somebody in stage four with a pitch designed for prospects in stage one will bore them to tears, and trying to sell to somebody in stage one with a pitch designed for stage three will leave them asking you to leave a brochure before they promptly forget about you.

To be successful with the widest range of clients and prospects, it's imperative to have a separate strategy and game plan to work with prospects in each stage, and to quickly and accurately assess which stage your client/prospect is in before you move into your approach. Great salespeople do this naturally, and the rest flounder amusingly. Let's work backwards, starting with stage four.

Stage Four: "Shut up and take my money!"

At this stage, customers know almost as much as we do about the product or service they're buying from us and probably more about our competitors' versions of those products. They know the problem they have, and they know that what you're selling is the perfect solution. What they want here is an order taker; they've decided to buy your product, and the only questions they'll be asking will fall into one of three categories:

1. Perfunctory questions that are fairly self-evident, mostly to cover their backsides: "Have you done this kind of work before?" or "This is covered under your company-wide refund policy, right?" or "It's not going to explode two days after the warranty expires, is it?"

2. Bargain-seeking questions. Given that they've likely researched your offerings against all your competitors, they may probe to see how much leeway you have between your stated prices and the prices you'll accept, using gambits such as, "I was just talking to your competitor, and they told me they'd beat your price by 10 percent." Obviously, if you don't have a good sense of your competitor's offerings, this could cause you some trouble, but typically you can maneuver around this stage by explaining the differences in your offerings and service levels.

3. Testing questions. In some cases, customers who know exactly what they want to buy will want to

make sure that you're the right person to buy it from. This happens rarely when they're buying a pack of gum and more often when they're buying six- and seven-figure service contracts. They know they want what you're offering, and they're willing to pay, but they're going to ask you questions to make sure your answers make sense. In effect, they're giving you every opportunity to hang yourself by demonstrating that you have misunderstood some part of the requirements or to catch you obfuscating the truth. If you do, nothing will save the sale from the wary buyer.

We all have stories about this third type of question, whether we were on the right or wrong side. You were buying a computer and nearly took the associate's head off when he told you that you should upgrade to the most expensive product on the shelf, even after you explained to him you only needed the machine for basic word processing and Internet connectivity, and that the "benefits" of the enhanced GPU that added $400 from the next best machine would go unnoticed by you.

Alternately, you might be uncomfortably remembering a time when you tried to bluster your way past a prospect's question with a "baffle them with bull" answer, only to be called to task for it.

Either way, it's no surprise that these kinds of questions exist. What is often overlooked, though, is that not being forthright in answering these questions will keep the prospect (and anybody they tell about their experience) from coming back to when they're in stage three or below with other products or services that you offer.

Aside from the third category of question, this is an incredibly straightforward phase. They want what you have, they've decided on you, and it's just a matter of asking them when they want delivery and how they'll be paying. If you have a company sales policy that requires you to do an elaborate song and dance for every prospect before you cut to the chase, you'll chase away these prospects pretty quickly. It's prospects in stage four for whom the phrase "Stop talking once you've made the sale" was created.

Stage Three: "I saw your ad, but I'm not interested."

In the pre-Internet age, this was the stage that most customers lived in. They had a clear picture of their problem, but couldn't choose who to purchase from. The main job of the salesperson in this stage is to explain why their product, service, or approach is better than the competition's.

Though less prevalent now than stage one, this is still an incredibly common stage for salespeople to meet prospects in. You'll recognize prospects in this stage when they say things such as, "So tell me why I should buy from you instead of [your biggest competitor]?" or "You know, I'm kind of on the fence about whether this is right for me—pitch me on why we need it."

Customers in this stage want to be reassured that what you're offering is the best way to solve their problem. Case studies, testimonials, and the ability to frame their problems (and what the post-solution world looks like) are all invaluable tools when working with prospects in this stage. If you try to skip over these, and operate as if they were in stage four, you're going to lose the sale pretty quickly by being seen as a pushy salesperson who is too eager to get the commission, rather than ensure you're helping them make the right choice.

If your sales team doesn't have a good understanding of the most common issues your prospects face, and how each of your solutions map onto those issues, then you're going to be losing a lot of revenue that would otherwise have been yours, because even in our brave new post-Internet world, there are still plenty of consumers who need you to show them why dealing with you is the wise choice.

Stage Two: "I've got a problem that I'll pay you to fix, but I have no idea your product exists!"

In this stage, prospects know that they could be doing better, but they have no idea how exactly to get to "better." They can't even really define their problem, let alone know what product/service will solve it. They simply have a general feeling of unease and a sense that things could (and should!) be better.

This is the stage where there is the highest potential to bring value to your prospects and customers, and paradoxically, where they're least likely to be receptive to your efforts to help in the information age. The reasoning for that is simple, if often misguided. People feel like if there was already a way to solve their concern, they would have found it and implemented it. The fact that they haven't been able to find a solution means that the solution either can't be readily found or that what is offered as a solution just won't work.

A compound effect here is that poor experiences in dealing with salespeople for purchases when they were in stages four and three lead prospects to doubt how much they can trust salespeople to have their best interest at heart. That trust must be fully granted before they'll be open to working with prospects when they're in this stage.

One trap that's easy for salespeople to fall into is to treat prospects in this stage as if they were in stage three. They think, "If I just present them with compelling arguments to show them that our service is the best, surely they'll buy it!" But at this stage, prospects don't believe that an existing product or service will solve their problem because they haven't defined their problem in concrete terms.

The key to success at this stage is to help the prospect frame their problem in a way that generates this response from prospects: "Yes, that's exactly it! I didn't have the words for it before." Only once the problem has been adequately defined will the prospect even be willing to hear about solutions to it.

Stage One: "Who would ever buy that and why?"

We all know and love Apple's famous tablet, but let's face it: most of us use it to jot down notes, play silly games, and try not to think too hard about why we spent this much money for something that's not exactly a world-beating game changer.

I am, of course, referring to the Apple Newton, which is more remembered as a punch line than as the grand-daddy of iPad and tablet computing as a whole.

The Newton faced the same challenge that anybody trying to sell a stage one prospect has—namely, that the very reason for the product's existence wasn't clear, and there was no compelling argument to be made about why you needed to buy it.

There's not much to say about trying to sell to prospects in this stage. If you're unfortunate enough to be so early to your market that most of your prospects are in stage one, then our only advice is to find an unlimited source of funding to create the market from scratch, or get the hell out until a better funded company paves the way for you.

Worlds Apart: Buying vs. Being Sold

Unfortunately, our prospects and clients don't come with handy labels letting us know which stage they're in. As each stage entails such a different buying process (and hence a different set of needs from your salespeople), it's imperative that the first step of any selling process is to identify what stage the buyer is in, and to find a way to tactfully find out what they need from us.

The single most effective way I've ever learned to do this was from my mentor, Alan Weiss, who taught me to start every meeting by asking, "So, before we get started, I'm curious, why did you agree to meet with me today?" and to not accept a pat answer.

> **Prospect:** "Because you asked to meet with me."
>
> **Salesperson:** "Oh, come on. You're obviously a busy person. I tripped over 15 people on my way here who would have loved to meet with you, so what made you decide to take 15 minutes out of your day to talk to me?"

As professionals, we all understand that our prospects and clients aren't lying awake at night trying to devise ways to put more money in our pockets. They have their own concerns, worries, triumphs, and goals to keep them busy. The fact that they're talking to you means that they have some hope, however small, that you will be able to provide value. Your first job is to understand what that value means to them, and to determine what stage of customer readiness they're in. Make no mistake, this is one of the most valuable lessons we've adopted and preached to our clients across the board. Prospective customers and existing customers alike don't wake up every morning wondering how to give your business more money!

The responses from your prospects here may run the gamut from, "You sell the Widget Title XII; I need seven of them by Monday, so where do I sign?" to, "I read an article by your company and it resonated with me. I don't know how, but I think you might be able to help us out around here."

Whatever they say, it will help you understand which stage they're in, and more importantly, allow you to start the conversation focused on what they're thinking, what they need, and what they hope to get from you.

Contrast a discussion that starts this way with the pitch-fests we've all politely struggled through, spending an interminable time listening to the pre-canned presentation while valiantly avoiding shouting at the salesperson, "What in blue hell does this have to do with me?!" Invariably, these pitches end with us asking them to leave a brochure or email us more information, just so we can get them out of our office.

The most powerful thing about starting prospect meetings with this question, in my mind, is that it serves as a valuable reminder: we're there to help them buy, not to sell them.

The Element of Trust

The amount of trust required in a relationship between your salespeople and your prospects can vary tremendously depending on what stage of readiness they're in, what the product/service being purchased is, and what factors external to the salesperson/buyer relationship are in place.

We all understand this at some level. If you're buying a pack of gum from a grocery store, it really doesn't matter what you think of the person behind the counter. Because you walked in and picked the pack of gum that you wanted, there was no outside pressure on you to buy something that wasn't in your best interest. At the end of the transaction, you will be handed a receipt that serves as proof that you paid, and the gum is legally yours. There is very little in this situation that calls for any trust whatsoever, no matter how upstanding or ethically dubious the person behind the counter is.

Now, contrast this with hiring a lawyer. How can you judge the effectiveness between four different candidates, each charging twice as much per hour as the last? Sure, you can assume that price equals quality and you can hire the most expensive one, but there is nothing stopping the least effective lawyer from quoting you the highest price.

You could interview all of them and see which one you like best. But you're not hiring a friend; you're hiring a lawyer, ostensibly to take advantage of their expertise.

You could use their past results as a guide post, and hire the one with the most experience in the area you have the most need. This is the best strategy so far, but it means that you will overlook very talented and capable individuals who are near the start of their career, and you run the risk of being sold on the successes of the older lawyer, without necessarily hearing about their failures.

It seems clear that in the case of buying a pack of gum, you are in stage four. When you are hiring a lawyer, you are typically in stage two or three. In each of these stages, the amount that you need to trust the other party increases exponentially.

This may seem like an obvious point, but the implications to selling are tremendous.

In his wonderful book *The Speed of Trust*, Stephen M.R. Covey proposes that a trusting relationship is built on four foundations:

1. Integrity.
2. Intent.
3. Capabilities.
4. Results.

Integrity is important no matter what stage we are in. At some basic level, I have to trust that you're not going to rob me. But in stage four, this is the only one of the trust foundations that we need to worry about.

In stage three, we need to add in the element of intent. By this, I mean that we have to trust that the person we're dealing with is telling us the truth, as well as guiding us down a path that is in our best interest. Because we are weighing multiple options, but have a pretty good idea of the type or category of purchase we are looking to make, it becomes much easier to accept the influence of a salesperson when we have a genuine belief that they have our best interest at heart.

Here's an interesting question to ask your sales team: what would cause you to tell this prospect that they should not buy from us?

How anybody in your company answers this question is extremely telling. If they can't think of a valid reason for somebody to not buy your product, there is very little chance that they will ever be able to act with the buyer's best interest at heart.

In stage two, our capabilities and history of results with similar customer situations become increasingly important. Recall that in this stage, the prospect is completely unaware that there is a pre-existing solution to the problem they had, and they may not even be able to articulate the actual problem they're facing. Unless we can demonstrate that we have high integrity, have their best interest at heart, and have the required capability and previous successes to demonstrate to them that we do indeed understand what they need and can provide it for them, it will be very hard for them to accept our influence.

My mentor, Alan Weiss, has often said that trying to push a deal before there is a solid element of trust in place is completely counterproductive. As he puts it, with no trust, your prospect won't even accept a compliment from you. With trust in place, they can accept criticism as well as help.

Of course, it's not impossible to sell somebody without having a strong foundation of trust. There is an entire industry built on teaching salespeople how to close the deal, how to use psychological tactics in order to make people feel pressured into purchasing, with little to no regard for their best interest. I probably don't need to spend too many words cataloging the differences that these two approaches have in creating content vs. dissatisfied customers down the road, do I?

Happy Endings Equal Happy Customers

In *Authentic Happiness: Using the New Positive Psychology to Realize Your Potential for Lasting Fulfillment*, Dr. Martin Seligman writes about a medical experiment that elucidates a powerful business lesson, and one that is immensely powerful for our learning in this book.

[In one experiment], 682 patients were randomly assigned to either the usual colonoscopy or to a procedure in which one extra minute was added on at the end, but with the colonoscope not moving. A stationary colonoscope provides a less uncomfortable final minute than what went before, but it does add one extra minute of discomfort. The added minute means, of course, that this group gets more total pain than the routine group. Because their experience ends relatively well, however, their memory of the episode is much rosier and, astonishingly, they are more willing to undergo the procedure again than the routine group. In your own life, you should take particular care with endings, for their color will forever tinge your memory

of the entire relationship and your willingness
to re-enter it.[1]

Of course, the concept of the "end" of an experience
is tricky to measure, isn't it? It's like the old philosopher's
trick of saying that you can't really tell if you're happy
until after you're dead, because a life can only be measured in its totality.

This is bunk in philosophy, and it's bunk here. For our
purposes, we can define an "ending" as the most recent
experience that a client has with you. It's a fitting definition, too, because if that last experience is bad, it may
very well be the ending of their relationship with you.

Think about that for a moment. Basically, what it's
telling us is that even a wonderful vacation can be ruined
on the last day of the vacation. The customer is more likely to remember the negative experience as opposed to the
positive experience. A fine meal at a fancy restaurant can
be ruined and forgotten by a negative experience when
trying to pay the bill. How can you ensure that your customer experiences start and end as well as possible?

Of course, it's easy to see how this applies on a cruise
or at a restaurant. But what about day to day in other businesses, where it's much harder to define an experience?
In the rest of this chapter, you'll find three sample situations; your task is to describe how you would end, resolve,
add to, or rectify the situation. You don't need to write
in the book, but you can use these with your team and
scenarios to discuss how they might respond. Keeping in
mind that endings are one of the most powerful parts of

the customer experience, how would you end the following situations?

Situation 1

Your customer and his wife have stayed at your hotel for the last seven days. They had a fantastic experience and were thrilled with the entire vacation. But the experience ended poorly. The night before leaving, they had the concierge book a car to take them to the airport. They booked the car for 6 a.m., but the concierge booked it for 6 p.m. When they arrived in the lobby at 5:45 a.m., there was no car, and nobody at the concierge desk.

You tried calling the car service, but got an automated machine asking you to leave a message. You checked Uber for the customer, but found the nearest car was showing as 25 minutes away. You called the local taxi company, but they had nothing available. Your shuttle driver just left with another group on the way to the airport.

What do you do?

Situation 2

You're the sales manager of a car dealership for a prestigious brand. One of your youngest sales reps is leading the charge for most cars sold during the past month! He has an uncanny ability to create rapport with customers and sell cars.

On this particular occasion, a family of four is picking up their new car. He doesn't realize the family is there when he makes a rude comment about the man's wife. The couple pretends they didn't hear the comment, but you know they did and the experience has gone from great to awkward.

What will you do?

Situation 3

You're the president of a commercial property developer. You've worked for the last 25 years to build a portfolio in the billions, and you pride yourself on your customer service. Your sales team has spent the last six months wooing a new tenant. They've finally signed on the dotted line, and your sales team gets the customary celebration party.

As the president of the company, you think all is fine and the tenant is thrilled, until you finally hear from the tenant six months later. He's unhappy because, in his eyes, he was only given a set of keys to the complex and never heard from anyone on your team ever again. He's received no follow-up calls. Your sales team even neglected to give the tenant the welcome package that you'd spent so much time and money developing a few years back.

The tenant goes on to say that he'd also sent an email to his sales rep about a plumbing issue a month ago and he never heard a thing. He says in 20 years, he's never had a team spend so much time overpromising and underdelivering on so many levels. He's considering contesting the lease, but because he respects you, he wanted to discuss the situation with you first. The situation has escalated to where he's called you personally.

What do you do?

Chapter 4

Understanding Problem Children and Hungry Hippos

They May Be Loyal, But Are They Worth It?

"I would rather squat over a red-hot hibachi with fireworks up my butt than ever deal with you again!"

Though we've been asked to anonymize the story, we've got ample evidence those words were voiced by the CEO of a massive manufacturing firm while turning down a customer and a deal worth millions of dollars. There was no amount of money that made dealing with this customer worth the effort. In this chapter, we'll introduce two of the worst types of insatiable customers and how to deal with them. We'll also explain why your most loyal customers might be sapping you of profits and employee goodwill.

Do You Know Who to Fire?

It's one thing to fire an employee, but when is the best time to fire the customer? Why would someone want to get rid of a customer or client after you've worked so hard to get that customer in the first place?

Look, here it is in a nutshell: the customer is not always right. Now, before you either agree or disagree with the statement, let me tell you where I stand. Nearly everyone is familiar with Zappos, the mega online shoe retailer that was sold to Amazon for more than a billion dollars. Zappos, the brainchild of founder Tony Hsieh, took the idea of "wow" service to an entirely new level. Essentially, Zappos said to its employees something along the lines of, "Let's do whatever it takes to make keeping customers fun!" Whatever. Literally, whatever. And that is what they did. There have been dozens of classic stories. For example, some customer service calls have lasted 8–10 hours. In another example, a customer asked the representative to order a pizza, and in another classic example, a family who lost their mother found out after death she had a shoe addiction and had hundreds of pairs of unworn shoes in her closet. Zappos took them all back without question. It's a lot like the Nordstrom stories told years ago. In one classic example, Nordstrom apparently accepted a set of tires that a customer said they purchased at the store. Of course, Nordstrom had never sold tires.

Zappos has become a phenomenon in the world of customer service, but it has created a lot of problems. Believe me, I've seen them first hand in my work with many companies. You see, there have been literally thousands of books written by customer service experts on the topic of Zappos, and yet most of them haven't been working with organizations on the front lines, dealing with real situations and customer challenges. The most harmful issue with nearly every other marketing and customer service expert jumping on the "let's write a book about Zappos as a model of customer service" bandwagon is that the Zappos way isn't the only way. And there's a good chance it's not your way.

In fact, many often miss the crucial point that CEO Tony Hsieh has said himself: not every customer is worth keeping, which he discussed in his fantastic book *Delivering Happiness*. Tony suggested that any customer who was rude, vulgar, racist, or sexist in their discussions with his team was not welcome at Zappos.[1] This is a critical point most companies trying to embrace the Zappos model miss.

So, let's talk about a topic that most organizations are really afraid to discuss if we're really being honest: when to fire the customer, why, how to do it, and which customers you should fire. The reality is that organizations spend enormous amount of time, money, and resources on keeping customers and meeting unreasonable demands from customers who should be cut loose. In my first book, *Evergreen*, I devoted a similar chapter to this discussion because it's incredibly important for the future growth of your company.

How to Fire Bad Customers

Let's face it: our customers know more than ever before. We're living in profound times. Customers have not only gained more knowledge, but they've also gained more control and the ability to exert, expect, and demand the ways they'll do business with us. There's no such thing as "not knowing your pricing" because everyone has the same information. With a few clicks of the button, they've got it all. These are incredible times, and we've got to approach them by really thinking about the customer, how we service them, and their experience.

Look, we've all called customer service and wanted to throw our phone across the room. We've all heard the recording tell us our call is important to them and yet we all know the call wasn't really that important. If it was, I wouldn't have had to wait 27 minutes for a response. If it really was important, I wouldn't have had to re-tell my story four different times to four different people. We've all experienced the type of service that wants to make us drive off a cliff. Customer service in many organizations is broken, and in many cases, it can never be fixed on the front lines alone. They simply view it as something they can do and be good enough in to simply get by. But we're trying to show you a better way in this book, and one way is to work at ridding yourself of the bad customers to begin with. Remember the Bizarro World we introduced earlier in the book? Well, we had a lot of fun writing that because in many cases, companies continue to create their own customer-related issues by attracting the wrong customers and continue to serve them regardless of the customer's poor behavior.

Many companies farm out customer service to the cheapest places they can. If the phone is being answered, are they really providing any service? Truth be told, we all know just how many organizations would have been better offering no support! And for the love of all that is sacred in the world, we strongly suggest *never* outsourcing service to anyone outside your company, especially to folks without a direct profit and loss responsibility, but this doesn't mean you give away the farm to save every customer. It's more important to know which customers are worth keeping and which aren't. In a chapter coming shortly, I'll provide some tips and tricks your organization can use to provide common sense customer service—the type of customer service that resonates with customers and lets them know they were heard.

Let's start culling the herd. The Pareto principle, also known as the 80/20 rule, states that almost 80 percent of all results come from 20 percent of the action. Start here. Your data teams can show you who the top 20 percent of your customers are and who the bottom 80 percent are. Twenty percent of your customers are likely responsible for 80 percent of your profits. These are the customers we want to dedicate time, energy, and resources to when it comes to customer service. You'll also very quickly learn that 20 percent of your customers are creating 80 percent of your problems. These are the customers we want to fire. Let's be very clear here: we're not suggesting that you fire your customers based on how much revenue they bring you, but rather how many problems they're creating that *aren't your fault.*

Problem Children and Hungry Hippos

There are two types of really bad customers. These are the upper-echelon of the difficult camp. They're notoriously troublesome for most businesses and they hide in and amongst even some of your own most valuable clients. Allow me to introduce the two types of customers causing grief within your business. They are problem children and hungry hippos.

The Problem Child

We've all got them. We've all dealt with them. Any of us in business have had problem child customers. They're like little, malicious, troublesome kids who are constantly driving us just a little bit mad. The problem child is the term I use to describe the customer who is insatiable and can never be pleased, regardless of how well you do or how great your service is. She is, quite simply, never happy, for whatever reason. Some people are like this. Some have borderline personality disorders, but we all know problem children. You might even recognize them within your own family. Hey, it happens. They're constantly whining that people are taking advantage of them, and they're always complaining about one thing or another: too much salt; not enough salt; too peppery; too creamy; too slow; too fast; not enough; too much. No matter what you do, they simply can't be pleased, or even worse, they don't even give the illusion that they're remotely pleased. These customers complain. They complain a lot, and they're not afraid to do it.

It's usually pretty easy to identify the problem children in most businesses. They're almost always the lowest value, most price-sensitive customers you have. Problem children fall into the category of difficult. As I mentioned, more often than not, these people walk through the world with borderline personality disorders that make them genuinely bad customers. Every business has them. There are a gazillion of them. The best and most valuable thing you can do is recognize them and understand how to handle them. Understand that it's not you—it's them. There's very little chance these customers will ever exhibit the qualities of genuinely loyal customers. Now, here's the most important point of all: problem children can grow up to become hungry hippos. Let's introduce them now.

Hungry Hippos

I've got two daughters who are six and three years old at the time of this writing. Much to my surprise, I was thrilled to see them open a box at Christmas that contained a refreshed version of the popular 1980s game, Hungry Hungry Hippos. Do you remember the game? If not, here's how it works. Each player smacks a lever that causes their hippo to "eat" marbles. The player whose hippo eats the most marbles wins the game. Christmas Day went from a subtle mayhem to complete mayhem when the hippos finally made their appearance.

Every business has customers who we can define as hungry hippos, and we're all partially to blame because we keep giving them more and more marbles. Hungry hippos are the customers who may be pleased, they may even be happy to an extent, but they continue to zap your business of time, energy, resources, and even money. Yes, it's true. Even profitable customers aren't worth keeping if the customer is a hungry hippo. Although these customers may be considered "loyal" from a repeat visit/purchase standpoint, they're also intent on sucking you dry to ensure they get their money's worth.

Here's the perfect example of the typical hungry hippo. I was working with a restaurant client. We were engaged in a small project to do some customer service training for their staff. The phone rang and one person looked at the phone and said, "Oh, it's her." Someone else responded, "I'm not getting it." Then someone else said, "Well, there's no way I'm getting it." This went around the room and nobody wanted to answer the phone. When I asked the owner—my client—what the deal was, it turned out this was a *very* valuable, loyal customer, but she was rude, belligerent, and a giant pain in the butt.

Nobody wanted to serve her or talk to her, but because she spent so much money, she was allowed to keep treating the staff poorly. I helped them do a little analysis and it turned out she was a high-value customer, but was doing more damage than the money she was driving in terms of revenue. I had helped this client develop and implement a powerful loyalty system in place that allowed us to see she wasn't really as valuable as they first believed. But our analysis also involved looking at some of the obvious, but less tangible ways she was affecting the business. For example, nobody wanted to answer the phone when she called. Nobody wanted to serve her when she came in. The host didn't want to deal with her at the door, and we made a pretty simple assumption that the server stuck serving her was likely so upset that the other guests and customers' experiences were affected as well. The fact that nobody could pick up the phone was enough for me to tell my client they should get rid of this big ole' hippo. I coached the owner on speaking to her about her behavior and if it didn't change, she would be asked not to return. He wanted to try, he really did. But guess what happened? The behavior didn't change and she was eventually asked to leave and not return. Not every customer is worth keeping. This is a classic example of a problem child *and* a hungry hippo.

Go ahead and fire your hungry hippos and problem children. They're not worth your time, energy, or the expenses required to deal with them. But what about your least profitable customers? They are almost always worth your efforts! We'll talk about them next.

Which Customers Shouldn't You Fire?

Now that we've determined some customers need to be fired immediately, it's time to switch gears. During the past few years, everyone has been saying that you need to fire your least profitable customers. I disagree. If you start from a place where you recognize every customer entering your business has massive potential value, then we can't simply make a decision to fire customers who are low value. Instead, we need to focus on turning them into high-value customers. The current discourse on the topic suggests you have two types of customers: high-value customers and low-value customers. The "experts" have suggested our focus needs to be only on the high-value customers. This goes beyond your hungry hippos and problem children.

Your base of customers determines the value of your business, and the value of this asset is only equated based on the expected future value derived from profits and new business. Businesses can only gauge the value of their customer based on the expected future value. Likewise, a business will only know which customers to focus on and how based on segmenting and the data collected. Instead of firing customers simply based on value, I would suggest other criteria for firing customers—mainly, are they hungry hippos or problem children?

Classifying Demanding and Dissatisfied Customers

One of the biggest (and most understandable) mistakes that we see companies make is to try to shoehorn their *demanding* customers into either the hungry hippo or problem child categories, when in fact they're simply demanding the high standard which your company and branding have implicitly or explicitly promised.

Think back to the story about the high-end resort in Chapter 1. In it, the guest was greatly disappointed by the difference between the company promises and the reality that she experienced at the extremely pricey resort. She complained about not liking the food they'd stocked for her in the fridge, the appearance of the rooms vs. the pictures on the website, and the service level in general.

For any frontline employee or middle manager in the company who was on the receiving end of her complaint, the first temptation would naturally be to write her off.

"You just can't please some people!"

"Almost nobody else complains; she must be super picky."

"If she doesn't like it, she can go somewhere else next time."

If she were making these complaints about a stay at a Motel 6, we'd agree wholeheartedly! There, the complaints would have been drastically out of line with the expectations that could reasonably be held about the experience. It wasn't a Motel 6, though; it was a luxury property designed and marketed exclusively to create enchanting, over-the-top fantastic experiences for a premium price. (And to the management team's credit, the president met with my client to hear her concerns, to apologize, and to ask for her help in fixing the issues that she felt were the most disappointing. It would be hard to imagine a better response *after* a complaint than this!)

It's Not You, It's Me!

Put on your customer hat for a moment and think back to the last time you did business with a new provider where the experience was worse than you'd hoped (whether a supplier for your company, a contractor for your home, or even a new restaurant).

Did you find somebody to complain to, or did you just quietly resolve to stop doing business with them? More importantly, how do you think others would have reacted in the same situation?

What we've found in surveying customers and companies alike is that customers tend to be much more willing to "vote with their feet" than companies give them credit for. Our clients often tell us, "We've created an environment and relationships with our clients and prospects so they know they can tell us if there's any problem, and we will fix it for them and keep the relationship strong!" This, sadly, is wishful thinking on par with saying, "We've decided that our new corporate strategy is to hide in our offices and wish for success, eight hours per day, every day!"

Customers are under no obligation to put themselves into the awkward position of complaining about your poor service, just to help you get better. Much more often than not, they simply walk away silently, and if anybody asks them why they're leaving, they give a bland, useless excuse that doesn't bruise any egos such as, "I found it cheaper elsewhere," or "We're going in a different direction."

Side note: this is especially true in larger accounts, where you have the salesperson who most likely caused the account to be lost in the first place calling the (now ex-) client to ask what went wrong. For the most part, people are polite. It's awkward to say, "You didn't treat me the way I wanted to be treated." Instead, they find the gentlest way to let you down. It's the corporate version of "It's not you, it's me."

The Gift of Demanding and Dissatisfied Customers

It's for this reason that every customer complaint needs to be considered a gift. Sure, sometimes that gift is another sweater from a distant aunt who is far prouder of her knitting than her talent should allow. But more often than not, it's like being offered a breath mint—somebody is kindly and gently pointing out to you that you're not quite as put-together as you were hoping, and that person is helping you correct it before you embarrass yourself further.

Sometimes, one complaint helps to shed light on an issue that you had in place that is causing friction with your clients. Other times, it's hard to determine whether the complaint is a one-off from a problem child, or if it really does represent an opportunity for your company to change the way it does things to better serve all your clients.

In Chapter 5, we're going to recommend a tool and a discipline that involves tracking every complaint and every issue that you get, and regularly reviewing both the type of issue and how often it happens to find useful patterns. Sometimes, you'll find that what you had assumed was just the grumbling of a problem child is, in fact, a pervasive problem.

For example, if you have one person complaining about being charged too high a price, then it's their problem. If 30 percent of your complaints are about price, then you're doing a bad job in attracting the right customers with your marketing and pre-selling processes, or you're doing a bad job with their buying experiences, which leads them to assume they shouldn't be paying a premium. Knowing this, you can work with your sales and marketing teams in order to create experiences that more closely match the customers that you are trying to attract.

A newsletter reader of mine recently shared a story about a business that made some specific policy changes based on his complaint. He voiced his concerns and to his surprise, they responded and made positive change.

Here's what he had to say: "I take a spinning class at a local fitness club. It's popular. One morning, I realized that I wouldn't make the evening class at 5:45 p.m., so I called and cancelled. They have a no-show policy of charging you the full amount if you don't show up, which they should. But if you cancel within the 12-hour minimum, there is no charge. If you are inside the 12-hour minimum notice, they charge you 15 dollars."

Immediately after cancelling, David got the following "automated and canned response."

> *Hi David,*
>
> *We noticed that you have late cancelled for our studio class. Please note that we have a $15 cancellation fee for studio classes. In order to avoid such a charge, please cancel 12 hours in advance for a spin class and 24 hours for BodyBarre, Gravity, and Reformer.*

David was dismayed by the policy, so he emailed his concern.

> *Thanks for reaching out. However, I take offense to the late cancellation charge and I'll explain why. If I don't show up to a class that I was booked for without cancelling in advance, I completely agree you should charge me the full amount. However, when I call in the morning to cancel a class that evening (I gave seven hours-notice—12 hours would have been 5:45 a.m.), and you immediately sell the seat to someone else (which you did in this case, as you had a waiting list), then you have lost nothing, and therefore I cannot understand why I should be penalized. What am I being charged for if you are 100 percent sold out*

and made the sale on my bike? Is it just a punishment? It means you've earned $15 more than the entire class is worth at 100 percent capacity, and you have upset a client. Is it worth it? This is not about 15 dollars, I hope you realize. It's about the principle and customer service, and treating clients with some respect when you haven't lost a thing. I'd love to hear the logical explanation as to why you think I'm wrong.

Sincerely,

David

To David's surprise, the next day he got this wonderful response from his local spin class.

Hi David,

Sorry for the delay in getting back to you; I remember talking with you a few weeks ago. I hope all is well.

After reading your email, I believe you have brought up a justified argument. Starting next week, I will be implementing a new procedure that will prevent clients from being charged for late cancel if their seat was given to another client on the waitlist. I will make sure my staff refunds your $15 and adds an extra session onto your package for the inconvenience.

Have a great weekend.

Health Club Director

As you can see, sometimes the customer is wrong, and often the customer is right. We quite often don't see how our policies and procedures might be working against us to create feelings of ill-intent with our customers. We've both worked with numerous fitness facilities and understand the levels of churn and attrition these types of businesses have. Could something like this be the reason?

I love this example because it's a simple win-win for both the customer and company. The customer wins because he can cancel his class and knows the company isn't double-dipping by reselling seat and penalizing him, because let's face it (and put ourselves in the customer's shoes again), sometimes life happens and you need to cancel.

Identifying and Segmenting Your Customers

What separates problem children and hungry hippos from the rest of your customers are not the complaints they make, but rather whether they will be satisfied by reasonable efforts on your end to address their issues.

A new client who will go on to be in the top 5 percent of your customers with time may start the relationship by complaining about the lack of service they got, or the quality of the product you sold them. But if you genuinely address their issue and they accept that, then they definitely don't fall into the two "fireable" client categories.

Similarly, a new client may have no comment or complaint on the first 10 transactions and then suddenly start complaining about everything, seemingly complaining more to be vindictive than to try to create better experiences for themselves and other clients. Here are three simple tips for helping you address any customer's first complaint:

- ♻ Treat every customer's first complaint as if it was served to you on a silver platter.

- ♻ Determine if this is a new issue or if somebody else has commented about it.

  - If it's new, ask yourself and your team if there's anything you can do to correct it.

  - If it's not new, re-examine why it hasn't been corrected yet.

- ♻ Have somebody on your team follow up with them personally (it is okay to send an auto-generated message to them to let them know when to expect a response, but not to respond solely with autogenerated or form responses).

Of course, if it's not their first complaint, and if it's not an issue that you feel is worth resolving, then you may need to move to the next step: resetting the expectations with that customer or ultimately firing them.

How to Fire Bad Clients

One disgruntled keyboard cowboy took it to the interwebs to share his disbelief that he had been banned from shopping at Amazon.com due to negative complaints and excessive returns. He was sharing this on an online message board dedicated to sharing and discussing how to copy and burn blu-ray discs.

It's not hard to read between the lines here and make a good guess at what was happening, especially in the days before Netflix streaming. It was very common to see people copying DVDs and blu-rays either for their personal use or for resale. In this case, it would be reasonable to guess that the individual in question was putting extra financial strain on Amazon by purchasing the DVD, copying it, and then making Amazon foot the return costs.

In this case, it's hard to fault Amazon for their decision. But a similar conundrum is faced by companies every day even without the larcenous intent of the customer. Namely, the customer's actions are making them unprofitable or unpleasant to work with, so is there any option but to fire them or continue taking their abuse?

We have seen some companies engage successfully in a middle path between these two options, and that is *renegotiating the terms of the relationship*. In short, this has three components:

1. Identify a behavior or set of behaviors that is causing friction between you and the customer.

2. Identify what would have to change in order to make you want to continue serving that customer.

3. Communicate the required changes to the customer, and enforce the terms of the new relationship.

To make this apparent, let's give an example (anonymized and based on a colleague's experience).

Joe runs a fairly successful direct marketing company, where he sells specialty items to people through a combination of physical catalogs and an online retail presence. For simplicity's sake, let's use a baseline of $50 million in annual sales, turning a profit of $1 million/year.

Joe has identified that the single biggest source of recoverable expenses that he has is due to product returns (part of what makes his business so appealing is that customers are given 90 days to return their purchase, no questions asked, with the company paying for the shipping costs).

Of course, it's more than shipping costs. There are credit card refund expenses, additional time, and logistics resources required to handle the reshelving and restocking, and of course the inevitable waste when seasonal items are returned that can't go back into circulation, even with a "refurbished" tag on them.

When Joe and his team look at their purchase and return statistics, they find that a disproportionately huge percentage of returns are coming from a tiny group of their customers. Some may be malicious, but most are likely unaware that their behavior is far outside the norm, and some may even have compulsive behavior disorders.

Whatever the cause, it quickly became clear that if the company were to "fire" these customers, they'd lose about $1 million in gross sales, but save $250,000 in operating costs. In other words, their gross sales would go down by 2 percent, but their profits would go up by 25 percent.

Of course, the best option of all would be to not have to fire the clients, but rather to stop them from engaging in the egregious refunds and returns.

So, what Joe and his team did was to flag all the accounts of these clients and send them a letter laying out for them the choice between continuing to be a customer, but limiting the number of refunds they were allowed to claim per year, or being banned from doing business with the company.

Further, on the next purchase attempt, Joe had trained his staff to bring up the topic to the client and let them know that if they wanted to proceed with the order, they had to agree to the new terms, namely, that they could only buy one item at a time, and if they returned any item, they wouldn't be allowed to be a customer anymore.

By doing so, the vast majority of customers decided to continue doing business with Joe's company, and of those, most stopped their refund addictions. Those who didn't were politely declined on all subsequent order attempts.

Part II

 **Chapter 5**

The Three Disciplines of Excellent Customer Service Organizations

How to Save Millions of Lives and Have Doctors Hate You

"They say that when all you have is a hammer, every problem starts to look like a nail. That's why carpenters make such poor babysitters."

—Cracked Magazine

In late 2006, Dr. Atul Gawande received a call from a representative of the World Health Organization, who had a small favor to ask him. They wanted to get his help in creating a program that would reduce the number of deaths and harm from surgeries and would be applicable to any hospital in the world.

They didn't really have a budget to do this, and the goal was outrageously aggressive. In 2004, surgeons were performing 230 million surgeries per year, and complications during surgery were causing serious harm. More than seven million people per year were being left disabled, and more than one million people per year were dying because of complications during surgery.

It seemed like an impossible task—the equivalent of telling an ambitious but troublesome child to dig a hole to the other side of the world so you can have a few minutes of peace.

Nevertheless, Dr. Gawande took on the challenge. What's more, he succeeded beyond anybody's wildest dreams.

He and his team found a way to reduce surgery-related injuries and deaths, not by one or two percentage points, but by almost half. It was something simple enough that it could be implemented in every operating theatre in the world, whether it was in the middle of a battlefield or at the Mayo Clinic.

Based on these numbers, this would lead to millions fewer people being left disabled, and hundreds of thousands of fewer deaths every year.

It's the kind of success rate that is impossible to ignore, even if you wanted to. So why did many doctors fight its implementation tooth and nail?

The title of Dr. Gawande's fantastic book about the program, *The Checklist Manifesto*, may provide a clue.

The intervention that Dr. Gawande and his team discovered wasn't complex. It wasn't a new surgical technique or a new drug. Instead, it was the use of a checklist during every surgery.[1]

Many doctors felt, in essence, that the checklist was beneath them. They felt it was an admission they needed help or weren't masters of their craft. They were arguing, "I spent four years doing my undergrad study, and then another two years of med school before I was allowed in a hospital. I've spent another five years working my butt off in hospitals all around the country, eating, sleeping, and breathing surgery. I know what I'm doing, and I don't need your little checklist to help. On top of that, every patient is different, and every surgery is different. You can't capture what I do in a checklist. It might be good for pilots and some other professions, but what I do is too complex to make it very helpful."

Remember, the study showed a reduction in deaths and injuries of between 30 and 47 percent in most cases. This wasn't a subtle improvement, but not even doctors are immune to the Lake Wobegon effect. "Sure, it may be helpful for other doctors who aren't as good as me," the dissenters seemed to be saying, "but it would just be a waste of my valuable time to put it into place."

Say what you will about McArthur Wheeler, but at least his overconfidence didn't kill anybody.

In this chapter, we'll look at tools almost as simple as the humble checklist that can have a similarly large impact on your customer service efforts.

It's a Jungle Out There!

The woman looked furious, as she waved a pair of jeans that had noticeable grass stains on them vigorously at Claire.

"I bought these here less than two weeks ago, and that sign on the wall right there says I have a 30-day return period! If you don't give me my money back right now, I'm going to sue you and the store and put everyone here out of business!"

It was Claire's third day on the job, and she was now quite certain that she was not ready for this.

"Ma'am? Ma'am…um…please, ma'am, our policy is…um…our policy is to only accept returns on unworn items!"

"I don't care what your policy is! I'm telling you right now, you had better give me a full refund, or I swear I will never shop here again!"

Let's pause the scene here for a moment.

Is this a valid or an invalid complaint?

This is obviously a difficult customer, but in an ideal world, how would we want Claire to respond? Stated differently, from a corporate point of view, what is the best outcome that can be expected here?

Ninety-nine times out of one hundred, poor Claire would not have a successful outcome here. Her training during the previous two days would likely have consisted of being given the company policy manual upon being hired, perhaps as little as a day's training to familiarize her with all the products and basic expectations of dealing with the majority of customers, and then being left mostly to her own devices until something went wrong, at which point she would have a very uncomfortable chat with her manager.

Luckily for Claire, this is the other one time. She's not on the sales floor right now and not actually dealing with an irate customer. Instead, it's her manager shaking these stained pants at her, and this is the third time this morning they have rehearsed this scene.

"That's good, Claire! You are absolutely right on our policy, but we still need to work on what you say to our client before you get there. Remember, it's not enough for us to be right. We also need to be sensitive to our clients' needs, and ensure they feel like we're on their side. Until they stop believing that we personally are their enemy, it really won't matter what we say. Let's try again, and start out with some of the approaches for initially engaging with the visibly irate customer."

The Three Disciplines of Excellent Customer Service Organizations

There are a lot of ways to be excellent in any field, and customer service is no exception. We can't give you a detailed listing of everything you must do to be great at customer service because the exact elements and details are going to be different on an industry-by-industry, and even a company-by-company, basis.

What we can do is point to three high-level patterns and behaviors that seem to be shared by the companies we have worked with that have had the greatest success minimizing the number of displeased customers they have, as well as in dealing with those customers when they appear.

1. Developing a living script book of possible issues and best responses.

2. Prioritized and regular role-playing training.

3. Using internal benchmarking to identify problem areas and bright spots.

The rest of this chapter will focus on how to develop a useful script book and how to incorporate role-playing training into your customer service efforts.

The next chapter will focus solely on setting up an internal benchmarking program and demonstrating how doing so will make it easier than ever before for you to serve all your customers (including those who start out demanding, dissatisfied, or disagreeable).

The Simplest Truth About Customer Service

Whenever you're dealing with a dissatisfied customer, it can feel like there are a million things that can go wrong. We've heard people refer to it as trying to juggle chainsaws while tightrope walking. For customer service managers in companies or industries where there are a lot of irate customers, there's a constant challenge of trying to find and keep people who can do this tightrope juggling because they rightly recognize that effectively calming angry customers and creating positive resolutions is an incredibly valuable skill.

Without taking away anything from the great work that is done by these super-service representatives, we've found that this characterization is only half right. Yes, you can solve the problem by having extremely high hiring standards and finding people who can naturally find the balance between giving the customers what they need *and* staying within the bounds of corporate policy. It's an inefficient approach that relies on stumbling on the absolute best candidates during the hiring process and praying that they stick around.

Alternately, you can solve the problem by recognizing and taking action on a simple, universal truth:

> *There are a finite number of reasonable complaints or issues that your staff will ever face, and you can prepare them for these encounters before they happen.*

Don't Worry About the Alien Invasion

My mentor Alan Weiss often shares a wonderful example to drive this point home for salespeople.

To paraphrase, he says that you will absolutely be talking to people who tell you that your price is too high. They will tell you that they don't have time to meet with you or don't have time to implement the strategies you suggest.

They will tell you that they love everything you've said, but they don't have the budget. They will tell you that they tried something similar once and it failed, and they will question why your method will be any better.

If you're not ready to answer these objections, then you are being negligent and you deserve to lose the business. This sounds harsh, but it's true. There are really only a handful of things a client can say, or a finite number of objections your people can hear. You'd better be ready for them.

You will never in your career talk to somebody who tells you they'd love to do business with you, but they can't because they're going to be beamed up to the alien mother-ship at 7:45 a.m. tomorrow morning, and so they can't in good faith make any financial commitments. If you do hear this, just politely excuse yourself and run away as quickly as possible.

It's easy to get overwhelmed with the feeling that there are an infinite number of possible situations that we could be confronted with, and that it's impossible to prepare, so the only hope we have is to find people who are immensely adaptable and naturally talented.

Instead, we suggest there is a much more practical way to approach these challenges. My grandfather often uses the line, "If I only had a dime for every time..." I've never had a reason to use that phrase until now. If I only had a dime for every time I've worked with teams—sales, service, customer-facing—and they say, "What if?" What if the customer said this? What if the customer said that?

What if the customer did this? This is certainly *a* solution to the challenges of dealing with dissatisfied and angry customers, but it is not *the only* solution. In fact, we'll propose that it's actually an extremely suboptimal solution.

Just Follow the Script

If it's true that there are a finite number of situations that your staff will deal with, then it seems equally true that there are only a finite number of "best" responses.

Let's be clear: we're not suggesting that there's a direct one-to-one mapping of "Issue leads to Best Answer." If this was the case, we wouldn't need customer service at all. We could just have a robot placed to accept abuse and spit out the "best" answer.

What we are suggesting is that it's always possible to identify 5–10 great responses to almost every customer service issue you're likely to face and to train your staff to choose the appropriate response based on the customer in front of them and their own comfort levels. Process is everything in our world, and if your people aren't prepared for the most common scenarios, then you deserve the one-star Yelp review. You deserve the social media blowback. I remember how I felt when my mentor told me if I wasn't prepared, then I didn't deserve the business, but he was right.

By pre-identifying the likely scenarios, then identifying the best responses to those scenarios, and creating an environment that emphasizes the importance of practicing these responses until they are natural, the challenges of dealing with dissatisfied customers transforms from juggling chainsaws on a tightrope to walking in a straight line without falling down. Sure, they both take some training, but the latter is unquestionably easier than the former.

Resistance Is Futile

Typically, when we recommend the adoption of a company-wide script book for any group (usually either sales or customer service), we're met with more resistance than if we'd suggested that everybody take an 80 percent pay cut. That's not an exaggeration. People *hate* the idea of formalized scripts and "right answers" to common and uncommon situations. Much like the surgeons at the start of the chapter, they'll tell us about the complexity of dealing with "real people" (instead of fake people, we suppose), and how there are just too many variables in their day-to-day jobs to make the process of using a script book worthwhile. They say things such as, "I've been doing customer service for 25 years! Every situation is different!" or, "I've been in sales for 30 years! No script book is going to help me."

One of the most common objections we face when talking to companies about implementing a script book is, "If it was just a matter of remembering the right answer, why would we be needed at all?" Of course, because it's common, and we practice what we preach, we have a few scripted answers prepared.

☝ "For the same reasons that pilots have checklists for literally everything—to allow them to take their mind off problems that they don't need to worry about, and instead invest their mental effort and energy into doing what they're best at—flying the plane and getting everybody to their destinations safely and comfortably. In your role, script books would allow you to resolve customer issues more quickly, more frequently, and with the customers feeling better about the outcome." *A soft response.*

☝ "Let me ask you something. When somebody asks you, 'How are you doing?' do you take 40 seconds to think about it, and then spend two minutes telling them about everything that's going on in your world, or do you say, 'Fine, thanks, and you?' The latter is a scripted answer. It's a script that everybody in our society knows and follows. If you follow that script, why would it be hard to follow a script at work?" *A bit tougher.*

☝ "You know, it's interesting that you say that. Did you know that in 2006, researchers found a way for *every hospital in the world* to reduce the number of deaths during surgery by more than 30 percent, but that doctors everywhere fought it tooth and nail? It's a true story. A group of medical researchers found that by introducing a checklist at the start of surgical procedures, they could reduce deaths by 30 percent, and this was true whether the operation was happening in the middle of a battlefield or at the Mayo Clinic. But doctors said pretty much exactly what you're saying now: 'I'm too smart, I trained too hard, and my job is too complex to be boiled down to a checklist.' Their ego killed people, but yours is just costing the company a lot of money." *Boss response.*

Following up on the second response, scripts exist everywhere in our culture, and we all follow them without thinking most of the time. They ease social interactions and help society run smoothly. Certainly, they differ from region to region, but in general, we are all comfortable with the idea of "following the script" at a societal level.

Even at a personal level, though, we've noticed that individuals form their own scripts, often without thinking about it. Customer service representatives will hear the same complaints many, many times. In most cases, they recognize what answers work and what don't. They recognize that there are certain approaches that will help calm the customer down, and certain phrases that will set people off. With time, they start to use more of the former, and fewer of the latter, in order to make everybody's day easier.

The concept of a corporate script book just takes this process and expands it for the benefit of everybody. It's unlikely that any one representative will have stumbled on the exact right approaches and phrases that will be perfect for every complaint, but it's 100 percent certain that there is at least one representative in your company who has the best response to any given situation.

A script book creates a way for this information to be shared between everybody within the organization, rather than keeping it locked up in each representative's head.

Setting Up Your Script Book

After reading the above, it should be no surprise that one of the most common and most effective recommendations that we make with companies we work with is to implement a shared script book. Whether there are three or 3,000 people who will be contributing and benefiting from it, it's important to follow a few simple guidelines as you set it up.

We have developed a tool that makes this process as simple as possible for companies to put into place (which obviously utilizes these recommendations), but you can also implement it yourself by following the guidelines that follow.

Create separate script books for each functional area.

This seems like an obvious point, but often companies end up trying to put every potential interaction and answer into the same script book, which makes it hard to find the appropriate material for everybody.

For example, assume we have a sales script book, a customer service script book, and a script book for working with past customers and prospects. If all the potential

questions, complaints, objections, and scenarios are listed haphazardly, with five or 10 appropriate responses, it
quickly becomes a nightmare to find the right response
for the situation that you're interested in.

Instead, we want to have script books specifically for
our salespeople, a separate script book for our customer
service team, and a final script book for our marketing
team who is engaging in client retention and reactivation
efforts.

Keep your script books well organized into logical categories.

Once you have organized your script books by functional category, you will want to create situational-based
categories to put each individual scenario into.

For example, your customer service script book may
start with only three categories:

1. Complaints about product quality.

2. Complaints about level of service.

3. Complaints about company policy (refund, ex-
    change, warranty, etc.).

Our earlier example with Claire would obviously fall
into the third category here. This category could con-
tain dozens of individual complaints or scenarios, each of
which will have many appropriate responses.

It's worth mentioning at this point that when they
first start utilizing script books, some companies try to
enforce all members of their teams to memorize the entire script book. This is a counterproductive practice, and

we strongly urge against it. It is not important to know every answer to every possible situation. What is important is to know at least one response from the script book for each of the areas you are likely to face.

There is only one exception to this rule. We recommend that every script book, in every department, contains a section about the appropriate responses when you either do not know the answer or do not have the authority to help the client. Anytime a team member is faced with a situation where they don't know a scripted answer, they should use one of the answers from this section in order to buy themselves some time or space to find the answer the client needs. Obviously, once they are done helping the client, they should look in the script book to see if that situation was covered and learn the answer. If it does not exist in the script book, then they should suggest it as a future entry.

Allow everybody to suggest, but only a few to approve.

This is a somewhat unintuitive recommendation, but we have found that it is absolutely critical to separate the processes of recommending a new category or a new answer and officially including those recommendations in the script book. There are two core reasons why this separation is so important:

1. It forces management to consistently engage with the process of developing and maintaining the script book.

2. It ensures that all the answers are within the corporate boundaries.

Without consistent management engagement with the script book, the message that gets sent to everybody in the organization is, "This is not really that important." When everybody can see that management is paying attention to how they use the script book and using it themselves, acceptance and usage of the tool jumps dramatically. This is true for any intervention, of course, and we will revisit this concept in the next chapter when looking at the adoption of internal benchmarking metrics.

The second benefit should be obvious. It is imperative that you have a good idea of what is seen as acceptable practice from every one of your representatives. If they're suggesting script book additions that run contrary to how you want to present yourself to your clients, then it presents a great coaching opportunity (as well as ensuring that no others are trained to use the noncompliant scripts).

Allow all members to "vote up" any response, and to share their comments on each category, scenario, and response.

The purpose of having a shared script book is to find the best ideas for as many situations as possible and to ensure that everybody has access to those great ideas. A script book is a powerful first step in an institutional knowledge and learning program, which allows you to give every team member the benefit of the experience of every other member, both past and present.

Remember, the purpose of a script book isn't to create a hundred new things that each of your employees needs to memorize. It's not a mallet to smash them over the head with if they can't regurgitate the nine best answers to the customer saying, "I know the sale ended yesterday, but I want the discount anyway!" Instead, it is a resource that your people can use to find the response they're most comfortable with, fits the situation, and has been approved by senior management for that situation.

With this in mind, a simple listing of situations and responses quickly becomes almost meaningless. We want everybody involved to feel some sense of ownership with the script book, to feel that they're contributing to its development and its usefulness. In addition, of course, we want it to be as useful as possible.

The easiest way to do this is to encourage people to vote up the responses they have tried and which have worked for them. Encourage them to comment on what worked and what experiences they had as they experimented with new approaches. Pay attention to the times when people report that approaches failed, and either provide coaching to them or reconsider whether that approach is effective in that region or for your company as a whole.

A script book is a living document. It's not something that's set in stone and passed down through the ages. As it grows and evolves, you're capturing the insights of the people in your organization who are directly interacting with your clients every day. Used consistently and purposefully, it is one of the most powerful tools that you can introduce to your organization.

THE MOST IMPORTANT PART
OF ANY SCRIPT BOOK

There is one scenario that is so common, and so important, that we insist that everybody we work with practice the response, and more importantly, use it as often as possible. Whether we're doing one-on-one coaching or doing a keynote to a room filled with hundreds of people, if we're talking about script books, we insist that everybody practice their response to this scenario.

How do you respond when somebody asks you a question you don't know the answer to?

It's an innocuous scenario. We've all been in situations where we legitimately didn't know the answer, even when we thought we should. How we respond in this scenario is extremely telling to the person on the other side, and it's an important skill to have, even if you never interact with a customer.

The answer, of course, is to say some variation of, "That's a great question. I don't know the answer off the top of my head, but I can find out for you. I will give you a call with the answer tomorrow morning."

Note the elements here:

1. Immediately acknowledge that you don't know the answer.

2. Take responsibility for finding the answer.

3. Let them know when you'll get back to them with the answer.

4. Get back to them with the answer.

It's deceptively simple. We often hear people say, "This is a bare minimum of professionalism; why are you taking time to talk about this?"

The answer, of course, is because it is a bare minimum of professionalism. If people in your organization don't feel they can safely say, "I don't know," then you will have no idea what they are saying in the cases where they don't know, and that is a very dangerous path to walk.

Pay attention to the engagement rate of each team member.

Your script book will only be as good as your people make it, so it is vital that you promote the importance of contributing to it, either in the form of adding new situations, suggesting better responses to existing situations, voting up approaches that have worked for them, and commenting to share their experiences with various approaches.

At a more basic level, it's important that they actually review the script books, notice changes, and get new ideas on a regular basis.

Whatever the method you decide to use to implement your script book, make sure you can see reporting on these engagement metrics. With the Evergreen script book tool (contact us to learn more), we show engagement metrics such as:

- ⚫ How many times each employee logged-in in a given week.

- ⚫ How many suggestions, comments, and vote-ups each employee contributed in each week.

- ⚫ Which locations have the most activity on each of the previous metrics.

- ⚫ Which customer scenarios had the most engagement and discussion (this will give you an idea of what kinds of issues are most on the minds of your team members, in order to better understand where to focus coaching time and effort).

Making the Most of Your Script Book

Once you have your script book in place, you will start to see a huge difference in the quality and consistency of your people's responses to all your clients and their confidence in their ability to know how to respond in a huge variety of situations.

Of course, just knowing the right answer isn't enough. It has to be coupled with the right delivery; otherwise, angry customers will blow right past even your most meticulously crafted scripted responses.

We started this book by talking about the famous Robbers Cave study that led to the concept of "in-group vs. out-group," and in that chapter we looked at some of the effects of being in the "out-group." As a reminder, it's not pretty. When they start talking to you, dissatisfied and disagreeable customers will certainly see you, your company, and all your employees as part of the out-group, which means they are predisposed to dislike you and to dislike anything you say or do.

That's why it's crucial that before you do anything else, you do your best to move into that customer's in-group. We'll cover many more ideas on how to do this in a later chapter, but the basics are as follows:

1. Get them to see you as a human being (and not as a monster).

2. Have them believe you care about them.

3. Have them believe you've done your best to accommodate them.

These may sound like low bars to cross, but when somebody believes you're a member of an out-group, it can be very hard to even get past #1, let alone getting them beyond the next two steps. One of the best ways to develop the skills to do this in a variety of situations is to make heavy use of role-playing in your training process, both for new and experienced employees.

Before we get to how to structure role-play training, we need to spend a bit of time talking about the general practice of training.

Training Is a Process, Not an Event

All too frequently, we work with companies who treat training as if it's a once-a-year expense that they generously provide for their frontline staff. The truth is, of course, that training with no follow-up is next to useless.

As a side note, this is why we have to turn down every invitation we get to conduct "a training." It's not worth it to us because the client doesn't get value from it, and we pride ourselves on leaving clients in a better position than they were in before we worked together. We always need to get on the phone, or have a one-on-one discussion with the key executives to learn their specific outcomes (how will the organization be better off?). We'll fly to them if needed. But no, we won't talk to Sally, your training officer who has been charged with ordering donuts, finding a venue, and booking a speaker all within a ridiculous budget.

Training is a critical component for the long-term success of any individual, team, and company, but when done poorly, it's nothing more than a drain on resources and morale. In this section, we'll talk about the key reasons that most training efforts fail, and how you can do it right.

Imagine how scary driving would be if new drivers were trained in the same way that most frontline staff are. They would sit in a class for two or three hours being inundated with facts that they were unlikely to connect to any personal experience, then get thrown behind the wheel and told to do their best. If there were any problems, a friendly emergency crew would show up and take care of anybody left alive.

I don't know about you, but I would never leave my house if this was the case!

Especially when we're learning something new, repetition and personalized coaching are critical in our ability to develop our capabilities. People need the room to try new things, to have the freedom to fail often in low stakes and low-pressure environments, and to gradually build both their skills and their confidence before we can expect them to operate well in high-stress environments.

Talking to customer service staff about the training they receive and the expectations from their managers and head office, I'm often reminded of a piece of dialogue from the 1999 movie, *The Big Kahuna*:

> **Salesperson 1:** Throw me in the water and see if I can swim.
>
> **Salesperson 2:** I think you're missing the point here, Bob; we're about to throw you off a cliff and see if you can fly.[2]

We hope you'll consider this advice when you're looking to improve the customer service of your organization, and if you need some help, reach out; we're glad to help. Most important of all, we'll help ensure your dollars aren't wasted on "a training."

Prioritized and Regular Role-Playing Training

How long do you think it takes before you forget a new piece of information? More importantly for this book, how long do you think it takes before your frontline staff forget any training that you have given them? This is not a hypothetical question. There is a right answer, and it has been known since the late 1880s.

In 1885, Hermann Ebbinghaus published a paper which translates roughly to "Memory: A Contribution to Experimental Psychology."[3] In this paper, he describes an experiment that he ran on himself relating to his ability to memorize pieces of information and his retention of that information during periods ranging from minutes to months. The original work has been retested and replicated many times in the intervening 140 years, and almost all of its points came to the same somewhat disheartening conclusion: unless they engage in some form of review of the content, within 24 hours of learning something new, most people will have forgotten somewhere between 50–80 percent of what they were taught. By the time one month has gone by, those numbers rise to 95–97 percent.

There is a silver lining here. The research also unequivocally shows that participants who engaged in review of the material can cement their learning retention quite dramatically. The strongest effects come from a type of review called *spaced repetition learning*, where participants review new material very frequently after first learning, and then at longer intervals into the future.

For example, somebody learning the optimal response to a customer angrily demanding a refund because they saw a lower price on eBay will be much more likely to use this response if they review it at all the following times:

1 hour later

6 hours after that

1 day after that

3 days after that

5 days after that

10 days after that

20 days after that

Once a month forever after that

This is an example of spaced repetition learning, and outside of being able to apply a new skill directly on a day-to-day basis (which is like reviewing it every minute), it is the best way to learn new skills and information. Each time we review, we get to take a mini-quiz about whether we've retained the information, and we get feedback about what we are doing well and doing poorly.

This constant review and feedback allows us to avoid the Dunning-Kruger effect, and ensure we don't fool ourselves into believing that we have mastered something when our objective skill level is still low.

So, let's assume you know what the most prevalent customer complaints are. Because you're a clever company, you'll have lots of examples of situations in this category in your script book, a few great answers for each situation, and you'll use this information to create your customer service training.

Unless you make it easy for your staff to review this information, especially in the first few days after it was taught, by the time the following month rolls around, your staff will likely remember about 15 minutes' worth of the 8-hour training day that you had expended so many resources to create for them.

This type of review doesn't have to take long. In fact, after the first few review periods, it can go incredibly quickly. It's often enough to ask people what the correct response to the question is, and they will immediately have the correct answer jump to the top of their mind. It is only when long periods of time go by where they have no cause to think about the material that it will completely disappear from their minds.

It is also worth noting that this type of review is not just for rote memorization. It is also incredibly useful to help people remember all the steps you want them to take in more abstract situations. For example, later in this book, we will show you a quick and easy method to determine whether a complaint is valid, and suggestions on how to handle both valid and invalid complaints. You may teach this method to all your customer-facing staff, but we can guarantee you that if you don't create regular review of this material for them, it will not be effectively and consistently used at the front lines.

Role-Play Guidelines and Best Practices

Hopefully, you're convinced about the need for script books, spaced repetition learning to master the content, and role-playing to develop the skill of interacting with customers in a way that helps them bring you into their in-group so that they don't demonize you.

With that in mind, we're going to end the chapter with a few guidelines on how to create powerful and useful role-plays and share an example of a role-play exercise we often use to introduce just how effective this practice can be. Here are four suggestions to help.

Determine What the Goal of Each Session Is

Virtually every sport—no matter how diverse the rule set or objectives may be—shares one common element: the difference between great and world-class players is that the world-class players drill more often, and they drill with more focus than the merely good players.

By this point, the idea of the "10,000-hour rule" is almost a cliché. However, one of the areas of the original research that the popular press often ignores is that it's not just 10,000 hours of practice, but rather 10,000 hours of what is referred to as "deliberate practice." The difference is critical: you can call almost anything "practice," but deliberate practice has a very specific goal.

As a chess player, one practice session may be all about learning classical openings, another may be classic endgame puzzles, and yet another might be to determine the turning point in famous (and less famous) games.

It is not enough to simply play; focusing in on a single skill or objective and then putting focused effort on that is what creates growth.

The same is true in your role-plays. One session may be geared toward simply ensuring that your people have at least one "right" answer for multiple scenarios. Another might be dedicated toward building empathy skills and working to get into the customer's "in-group" (or at the very least, to not be seen as directly in the out-group).

Don't Just Try to Create "Gotchas"

It can be tempting for the person in the client role to try to find elaborate (and often unrealistic) "gotcha" moments, where they are simply trying to fluster or stump the person in the customer service role.

Most often, this involves the person in the client role responding in ways that are unnatural (for instance, "The Mother-ship is coming to beam me up tomorrow, so I need you to fix this right now!"). That's why it's so important for the person taking the client role to have the scene set for them (see the following example).

In other words, instead of playing "Nightmare Customer #4," it's much better to play the client as having real and understandable motivations.

For example, somebody who spent a little more money than they could afford might justify the experience, thinking it was worth it because of the experience and the high quality. They ended up experiencing a huge gap between their expectation and reality, and now feel cheated. They've got kids to get back to shortly, and don't have a lot of time, and need to get this resolved as quickly as possible.

Keep a Log of Sessions for Coaching Purposes

It is important to keep a log of role-play sessions, which highlights the specific skill that the individual was working on, how they performed, what insights (if any) they took away from the practice, whether their initial response was ideal or needed improvement, and any comments on the role-play from both people in client and customer service roles.

Keeping this log through time allows employees to see how far they've grown, situations that are consistently problematic for them, and it allows managers to see what areas need the most review and work.

Have Staff Report Whenever Reality Differs From Practice

The final step is to collect feedback from the customer service representatives about their experiences using the role-play lessons "in the wild." Whenever they run into a real-life scenario that is very different from what they'd practiced, they need to provide that feedback to their manager and to the organization as a whole. Much like with script books, the lessons from role-playing can be shared with everybody in the company so that everybody can get better.

Let's assume that a standard role-play starts out like this:

> **Customer:** "Go to hell; I hope you and your business are hit by a meteor today!"

> **Employee:** "I'm sorry to hear that, but have you considered it might be your fault?"

> **Customer:** "You're right, I was wrong all along!"

This may leave the employee feeling overconfident and not prepared for reality when they face their first customer wishing a meteor to fall on them. This employee will quickly learn that the role-play training and script book answer of "Have you considered it's your fault?" isn't particularly useful. However, if there is no feedback, then other employees will have to go through the same experience before they come to the same conclusions. This is clearly an inefficient process and can be easily avoided by sharing the feedback and experiences of all employees who work with customers.

Chapter 6

Internal Benchmarking

Here is a pop quiz to kick off Chapter 6. Consider the following questions:

What are the five most common complaints that your staff have dealt with in the past month?

Are those the same five complaints they have dealt with in the past quarter? What about the past year?

Of the last 100 complaints that have come in, how many have been resolved in a way that was satisfactory to both you and your client?

Answering questions such as these is a critical first step in knowing how to prioritize your training for all your frontline staff, as well as their managers who are going to be primarily responsible for coaching them and helping create the most positive resolutions for both sides.

Unfortunately, it is rare in many companies to find a systematic process of recording customer complaints and frequencies, let alone following up and recording the resolution.

We have worked with companies who have created dedicated systems solely for handling this; others have integrated it into their customer relationship management (CRM), and yet others have stored the information on spreadsheets that are combined on a monthly basis for corporate reporting. All of these methods can work, as long as they're being used consistently.

Every time we work with a company that has a system like this in place, they tell us the same thing: there are always one or two surprises in the top five most common complaints, and the frequency of complaints changes often enough that without this type of tracking and monitoring, they would never be able to anticipate what complaints are likely and to train their staff accordingly.

Whether you have one location or hundreds, whether you answer phone calls yourself or have dozens of agents in a call center, if you are serious about reducing the number of complaints you received, it is imperative that you track every complaint that comes in. Think about what we're suggesting here. It's a lot like what was shared earlier in the book when we introduced the hierarchy of horrors. It's hard to know where to improve if you don't know where you're messing up. But if you track, even for a short while, you'll start to find immediate areas to improve. I'm sure you've recognized by now that one of the core themes of our work is not to simply learn how to respond and deal with difficult customers because we've done something to tick them off. We're more interested in fixing your business and understanding *how* and *why* we're creating difficult customers, and what we can do to stop it.

Internal Benchmarking

We have asked you to consider putting practices into place that allow you to identify the most common trouble spots by location and by time period, and we've also suggested that when you are training people in how to address these trouble spots, you build in plenty of time for review. Well, what we have not yet considered is just how to determine what the optimal response is that you will be using to train your people.

Typically, we see companies engaging in one of three approaches to determine how they want all their frontline staff to handle any given situation:

1. A senior group of leaders within the organization reviews the data on most common and most likely problem types and carefully constructs the perfect response to each, which they then require all their staff to use.

2. Senior management takes a hands-off approach, insisting we hire great people and get out of their way! In this case, the appropriate response is determined at the customer service representative level or at most their supervisor.

3. A hybrid approach would be one in which senior management utilizes internal benchmarking tools to see which of their employees, managers, or locations are superstars compared to the company average and works with them to identify the differences in the superstar approach. At this point, the training for the rest of the company will be built around the best practices utilized by the superstar.

Although the third approach is undoubtedly the most effective, it can be hard for some companies to wrap their heads around both the tools that are required, as well as the initial time it takes to identify the best practices and disseminate them through the rest of the organization. Make no mistake—investing in these tools and approaches will be among the most effective interventions you can take to improve your relationships with difficult customers.

Internal benchmarking is simply the process of looking at everybody in your organization against a single metric, and using that to identify the ones who are far above average (the exemplars) and those below average who need more coaching and training. This might be looking at individuals, teams, stores, regions, or countries, depending on the size of your organization.

Once you've identified the group who is doing the best at the metric you're measuring, find all the ways you can pick their brains and transfer that talent elsewhere.

For example, a national restaurant chain may look at various performance metrics by manager, and if they find that 5 percent of their managers are consistently generating higher profits per table and higher tips per table, then it may well be worth flying them in to spend a week having them explain how they select their servers, how they train their people, and how they nurture, grow, and support their people.

Afterward, it may be instructional to take them to lower-performing restaurants and ask them to notice the difference in approaches between how they run their restaurant and how the low-performing manager runs theirs.

On the face of it, it sounds almost too easy. "Oh, sure, that's easy when you handpick the example. But how are we supposed to use that for customer service and dealing with dissatisfied customers, which is inherently subjective? I can't just peer into my crystal ball, magically know who's the best, and then base our strategy around that, can I?" It's a fair criticism; it can certainly be hard to generate objective data about difficult customer interactions, and even more so about successful handling of those interactions.

In this section, we will cover six tips for getting started with internal benchmarking and then discuss some potential problem spots to look for.

1. Start small, but start!

2. Make sure everybody understands why you are doing this.

3. Have a plan to handle resistance.

4. Spend time auditing, especially in the early days.

5. Celebrate when the system works.

6. Make it easier for your people to participate.

Start Small, But Start!

It will probably not surprise you to read that when we talked to organizations about getting better at dealing with their dissatisfied customers, our first question was invariably, "What are the five most common negative customer scenarios that your organization has dealt with in the past quarter and in the past year?"

Nine times out of 10, the answer to this question is, "We have no idea." No idea, really?

I bring this up not to shame anybody, but simply to acknowledge that for most organizations, any information will be better than what they have now.

Our first recommendation in these cases is to identify the smallest piece of information which, if you had it, would allow you to make better decisions in any area related to dealing with difficult customers (or as related to internal benchmarking, how you're contributing to creating dissatisfied customers).

What this piece of information is may vary wildly between industries, and even in companies within the same industry. Here are some examples of the minimum information content that was implemented as a first step by some clients:

- ⚒ Minutes per month per employee spent role-playing difficult situations with their managers to prepare for likely (or unlikely but high impact) customer service scenarios.

- ⚒ Ratio of time spent learning new material to time spent in review of previously taught material per employee.

- ⚒ Number of customer service incidents per store.

- ⚒ Ratio of incidents per location to successfully resolved incidents per location.

We'll suggest many ways to use this information later in the chapter. For now, it's enough for you to know the metric you want to start tracking, and then ensure it is being collected.

I want to pause here, because it's easy to gloss over the difficulty of that last piece of advice. It's easy to say, "Just figure out what you need, and then make sure you're collecting it!" If we were to leave it there, it would be no more useful than Warren Buffet's famous two rules of investing, which are: (1) Don't lose money, and (2) See rule 1.

Some companies will be lucky here and will already have systems in place collecting all the information they need to get started. For them, it's just a matter of amending their regular reports to include this. Those lucky readers can skip ahead to step 2; the rest of us need to spend some time talking about ways to start collecting the metrics we'll be measuring.

Remember, the most important element of this step is that we're starting. That means we're not going to get too hung up on getting perfect information from the get-go (if such a thing exists). Instead, we're going to get some information, which is still miles ahead of the none we're currently getting.

One of the easiest ways we can do this is to ask our people to do self-reporting. We can ask our retail store employees to record all negative customer interactions before they finish their shifts, giving brief details about the interactions, what the customer was irate about, and how they resolved the situation. For example, in a sales situation, when we're working with sales organizations to deal with customer objections more effectively, we'll build corporate script books by building a simple tool where sales reps can input the "most interesting objection" or "client interaction."

If, instead, our customers primarily reach out to us via a call center, then we are likely already tagging every call and complaint type. At this point, it's just a matter of aggregating this existing information into a better report.

But what if we're interested in training metrics instead? Again, we come back to the self-reporting—have each employee report how much time they're being asked to spend on training/review.

The motto for this step is start small. We're picking one thing we want to measure, and we're going to ask our people to self-report so we can collect the data and use it later. It doesn't get much smaller than that, but you'll be amazed at how quickly this first step starts paying dividends for you in terms of how well you understand what's happening, what challenges your people are facing, and how you can better equip them to serve your customers more effectively.

Skeptical readers may be wondering how we can trust all these self-reported numbers and worrying that the whole system will just be gamed and end up being useless. This is a valid concern, but it's not valid at this stage. We will cover this topic in some depth very shortly in step 4. Until then, your effort and concern is best spent figuring out how to roll this system out as quickly as possible.

Although these steps will be useful regardless of what you choose to measure, for the sake of giving clear examples, the rest of the steps will continue to consider the case of setting up reporting based around having all your people record every instance of a negative customer interaction and the resolutions to those interactions.

Make Sure Everybody Understands Why You Are Doing This

The value of internal benchmarking is that it allows us to identify bright spots within the organization and to find ways to take what they've learned and what they are doing well and disseminate it throughout the organization, making everybody better.

At its best, it helps you to allocate resources most effectively to help you continually improve and to recognize those who are doing outstanding work (as well as those who are making outstanding improvements).

At its worst, it is used solely as a bludgeon—a way to punish those who are in the bottom half of whatever metric you're looking at.

In a corporate culture that is already predisposed to walk on eggshells and not draw attention to itself, people will naturally assume you're only introducing internal benchmarking as a bludgeon, and so they will be reluctant to participate in the system. And as in most cases their participation is a requirement, it's critical to get this right.

So, you need to communicate to everybody in the organization why you're asking them to use some of their valuable time to give you even more reporting information. You also need to communicate to them that you are using this information to help them be more successful (and not just as a way to collect justifications to wipe out low-scoring employees or stores).

Here's what we've found when implementing these types of systems: it's important to use the information quickly to make policy decisions, and it's just as important to avoid using it to make personnel decisions until late in the adoption curve. So, by all means, use the information to change your training program; use it to reallocate resources between locations or regions; use it to find talented individuals and ask them to participate in some coaching and training to help others improve. But, do not use this to identify the lowest-scoring employees and fire them; do not use it to cut funding, or to beat up on managers and employees who are getting the lowest scores.

It is also critically important to communicate to people exactly how you want them to contribute to the system. Give them examples of the kinds of entries they might make, especially focusing on entries they may think are not important enough to enter.

Have a Plan to Handle Resistance

The first reaction of employees at all levels when they are asked to start doing additional self-reporting is to push back against it. They believe, and rightly so, that what is being asked of them is for an increase in their workload. There's no getting around the fact that implementing a system like this will at the very least create additional work for everybody. It may be the case that it will reduce their workload in the long-term, and it is almost certainly the case that it will dramatically improve your company's results in the long-term, but the answer to the question "How is this going to affect me tomorrow?" is "By adding a new task to your workload."

Answering this resistance is by no means a trivial task, and underestimating the pushback, or ignoring the reasons it exists, will almost always result in a failure to successfully implement.

The unofficial motto of middle managers everywhere when it comes to implementing new programs and change efforts is, "And this too shall pass." Their skepticism and frustration with what they see as a seemingly endless parade of one bright idea after another that will get in the way of their work is understandable, but it is without a doubt the single biggest reason that new initiatives fail.

The unfortunate truth is that from a middle manager's perspective, most change initiatives seem to follow a three-step process:

1. A senior manager reads a book or goes to a seminar and gets a great new idea for how to transform the business. For example, "We'll give our customers world-class service!"

2. They charge their direct reports and everybody underneath them with implementing this idea, without thinking through the practical, day-to-day details of how it will affect those direct reports.

3. After a suitable amount of time, the senior manager forgets about it and moves on to the next idea. At this point, their direct reports quietly stop doing any of the activities associated with the initiative.

Some ideas don't survive in a company because the idea is not a good fit within that company or within the market. In these cases, the middle managers are vindicated in their view that the sooner everybody forgets about it, the better. Much more frequently, though, good ideas are allowed to die because they are too low of a priority from a senior management point-of-view.

The cost of this resistance can be staggering. As a concrete example, consider one that we have seen in many sales teams (even in organizations that measure their revenue in billions of dollars per year): implementation of customer relationship management (CRM) systems.

At its most basic level, a CRM does three things:

1. It ensures that all leads and customers are in a central database (not hidden away in salespeople's little black books).

2. It records the interactions that salespeople have with clients and prospects, which give a way for managers and senior executives to see how salespeople are using their time.

3. It makes it easy to find prospects and customers before they fall through the cracks and ensures that as many deals as possible are won.

Without these systems, answering a question such as, "How many quotes do your salespeople forget about after fewer than three contacts?" or "What is the actual closing rate of prospects who make it to stage 3 of our sales process?" are impossible to answer. With these systems, the answers are at the fingertips of sales managers and company leaders alike.

To be clear, these things should be the bare minimum of what a company can expect from their sales team, but for decades, salespeople across every industry have somehow managed to curb the adoption of CRM systems by arguing, "Do you want us sitting in front of a computer like nerds or actually out selling?" Companies who didn't have a clear plan to handle resistance when trying to implement a CRM watched the effort die on the vine and remained unable to answer those most basic questions.

Let's consider our example of asking all front-facing staff to record any interactions with dissatisfied customers. We may ask them to record the following information:

1. Customer name.

2. Reason for customer dissatisfaction.

3. Whether the issue was resolved on the spot.

4. Short description of the incident and what the resolution was (or what steps are being taken to resolve it).

If we have all this information, we can look at any number of trends through time. For example:

- ⚬ How many incidents did Jane resolve on the spot this month vs. three months ago?

- ⚬ How many negative incidents did this store record this month vs. last month? Is it increasing or decreasing?

- ⚬ Did the training we gave in March impact the resolution of incidents in April and May? Did the effect last through the summer? (In other words, how effective was the training?)

- ⚬ Who are our "problem customers" who have incidents spanning many agents and locations?

⚏ What is the biggest reason for negative incidents, and what can we do to help prevent those?

When you know what information you're going to collect, and how you're going to use it, you are in a much better position to communicate the importance of the initiative throughout the organization and to handle resistance as it arises.

Spend Time Auditing, Especially in the Early Days

In the last step, we saw that when left to their own devices, most middle managers will be skeptical of new initiatives and processes, and just try to "wait them out." The best way to avoid this is to show them that you are paying attention to their usage of it.

This has multiple beneficial effects. First, it communicates that you care enough to pay attention, and so it signals that they should take it seriously. As a side note, if you don't care about it enough to follow up, then they are probably right to deduce that it's not really a high enough priority to be worth their time either.

Second, it allows you to very quickly find those who are using it as intended and praise their efforts. Similarly, it allows you to find those who are not adopting it, and coach and nudge them to participate. Again, your behavior here will be a powerful signal. If you show that their participation is voluntary, then many will simply refuse.

Finally, it allows you to quickly identify those who are gaming the system, and it gives you an opportunity to close the loopholes that allow for such gaming.

Celebrate When the System Works

The whole reason that we're going through the hard work of putting new systems into place is to allow senior management to make better decisions that will impact everybody in the organization to better serve the clients and customers.

It seems like that is too obvious a point to comment on, but I'm sure you have seen many instances where new programs were put into place, having been hailed as a silver bullet, only to be promptly forgotten by everybody within a very short timespan.

By asking people to put in the extra effort of self-reporting, we have asked them to invest in this initiative. It is only fair that we show them some return on that investment as quickly as we can.

This can be accomplished in a number of ways, but in this section we will focus on the two most common and effective ways that companies can celebrate the small wins of new systems and processes.

Observe and Publicize

The first is to keep an eye open for the people, departments, and locations where we can measure improvements from the time the system was put into place until now, and have them share their thoughts on how the new systems have helped them to do better.

Next, publicize the hell out of these accounts internally. The whole point of internal benchmarking is that we are finding proof from within our own organizations and our own people that the goals we are asking them to strive for are achievable.

It may seem strange to advise what is, in effect, a philosophy that says, "Put it into place and hope that it works." After all, what if we don't see any improvement?

The answer to that question is: we don't know. We've worked with hundreds of organizations and have found that in every one of them the old axiom of management holds true: "What gets measured gets done."

If you're measuring the number of complaints per store, and the number of resolutions per complaint for each one, you will find that almost all your stores will start to improve as you review the reports on a regular basis.

Some of these improvements will indeed come from gaming the system that we talked about in an earlier section. This is why the auditing we discussed there is so important. But that kind of gaming the system will actually be far less frequent than most managers worry about.

The rest of the improvements will come from shining light on what is actually happening and making everybody in the chain, from frontline staff all the way up to the senior managers looking at these reports, aware of what is happening. It's almost impossible to look at a week or a month's worth of these reports and not start to identify opportunities for improvement. What we have found time and again is that people want to do the best job they can. More often than not, what holds them back is uncertainty of what's expected, lack of training, too rigid processes that tie their hands, and in general, a feeling of disconnect between those who set the rules and those who are living with the consequences on a day-to-day basis.

By engaging with the information made available by this self-reporting exercise, your managers will find the places where each member of their staff is having individual problems and be able to better train them. Your regional manager will find which stores are having the biggest issues, and your senior managers will be able to identify the brightest stars throughout the company.

Once those stars have been identified, it would be negligent not to invest in spending as much time as required with them to identify what they are doing differently to be successful and to find ways to propagate those practices throughout the entire organization.

Let's be very clear here: it's certainly not reasonable to think that everybody will perform at the same level as your superstars. It is certainly feasible to take the best practices from the best performers, better tailor your training for everybody else, and see company-wide improvements of 1 or 2 percent. Your superstars will still be 10 to 15 percent better than the company average, but propagating that 1 to 2 percent increase across the entire company will have a tremendous impact.

Make It Easier for Your People to Participate

The final step in the process of rolling out an internal benchmarking program is to continually find ways to make it easier for your people to participate.

Perhaps you started the exercise by having every individual within a location email their manager with all the negative customer incidents they faced every day, having the manager compile that into a single document and categorize each of the complaints, and then emailing that to head office, where somebody else aggregates all the reports from all the managers into a shared company database.

Obviously, there are a lot of places in the system where we could reduce effort. For example, setting up an internal company website where each individual can login and record every incident will remove the aggregation steps at both the management and head office level. There will of course need to be some monitoring and category cleanup, but the workload required would be dramatically reduced.

We have seen far too many companies which were always planning to launch the next tool that would help them, only to have the launch date pushed one quarter at a time, until the internal support for it had pretty much dried up. It is far better to start this process, even if it is an ugly start, than to delay while waiting for a perfect solution.

The steps we've outlined in this chapter are all important, and you will see value from putting them into place.

But if you do nothing else, just remember the first step: *start*.

Chapter 7

Role-Play Exercises: Dealing With the Most Difficult Customers

Dealing With the Angry Customer

Everyone at some point will deal with customers who are fired up and angry over various issues. In other role-plays, we've given you examples to deal with customers who are disgruntled, dissatisfied, or overly demanding. Here, we will talk about how to diffuse a truly angry customer in any business and any type of customer service scenario.

Sometimes, when you know there's a problem with a customer, it can be a nagging, ongoing issue. But sometimes we rush to offer a solution when other times we need to slow down to speed up. What happens when we don't deal with the problems is we often end up letting the customer's grievance continue to grow until they finally explode. One of the best ways to deal with this type of customer is to be calm, cool, and collected. We're not trying to downplay how hard it is to act that way in these specific situations, but this is a great way and a wonderful tool to help diffuse and deescalate a very angry customer. If the customer has a valid complaint, we have to do our best to solve the problem. We have to give that problem the attention it deserves. If the complaint is invalid, but the customer is incredibly angry, we also need to do our best to resolve the issue accordingly. Just as we've done when dealing with valid or invalid complaints, there are a few simple rules that you can use to deal with the angry customer.

Six Simple Rules to Dealing With the Angry Customer

1. Apologize. There is nothing wrong with issuing an apology whether the complaint is valid or invalid. Even if the customer is angry and you're giving them an apology, this can still go a long way to diffuse the situation. Even if the complaint is wholly invalid, or if you can't apologize for the specific incident that the customer is angry about (for example, if there are legal considerations or policies in place to minimize liability), you can always apologize for the fact that the customer is feeling hurt, disrespected, or inconvenienced. In other words, remember they're human beings, not problems to deal with. They're trying to get through their days, just as you are trying to get through yours, and a little simple human compassion and understanding will go a long way to having them move you from the out-group (as an enemy) to their in-group (or, at the very least, to a neutral zone).

2. Be empathetic. Ask the customer to explain to you what happened and why they're so upset. Show them that you can relate and understand as to how and why they're feeling this way.

3. Stay calm. If you're dealing with an unhappy and angry customer, there's no doubt your nerves will be firing and your heart will be beating faster. Keep calm and stay the course. Repeat, if you have to, that you understand the customer, and you're there to help them. Show them you understand by listening attentively. Nothing feels like more of a slap in the face to a customer than to speak to a representative and have the feeling that they're not even listening to you.

4. Assure the customer a solution is coming. Remember, the customer's complaint may be valid and it may be completely invalid. We're still dealing with a very unhappy and angry customer at this point. We need to show the customer that we're listening and that we're already devising a solution to the problem. Involve the customer in the solution, and ask them how they would like to see the problem resolved.

5. Follow up! One of the critical mistakes of so many businesses is the lack of follow-up. Don't just assure the customer that a solution is coming! Tell them when you'll follow up, how you'll do it, and when they can expect to hear from you. Make sure that you do what you say you're going to do! (If you haven't guessed by now, that's one of the big themes in this book.)

6. Know when to let go. We told you earlier that even Zappos will fire a customer who is rude, racist, sexist, or vulgar. Just because you know how to diffuse the angry customer doesn't mean it's always worth doing—or that you should.

Try the following role-plays for practicing how to deal with the angry customer. You and a partner should take turns. Practice using the simple rules we've provided to disarm the customer.

Role-Play

Business scenario: You're a customer service representative for a large bank. You field phone calls on a daily basis, from a variety of customers. Some are angry and irate; others are calm, cool, and collected, but you've never had one quite like this customer. You answer the phone and the customer immediately starts telling you about a problem. She is so angry and distraught that you can barely understand what she's saying.

Customer scenario: You just received a letter in the mail informing you that you've not only missed payments due on your mortgage, but that the bank has filed legal proceedings against you! You've been paying your bill for years on autopilot, and you've never had a problem. You've been a customer of this bank for years. You've never missed a payment and you've never been late. Last week, you tried to buy something, and then you tried to buy something a few days later. Both times, your credit card was rejected. You didn't think anything of it until this letter arrived. The letter informs you to call this number if you have any further questions. At this point, you're so angry and upset that you don't know what to do. You settle down just enough to call the number listed on the letter.

Curveball: For a curveball, try becoming overly belligerent with the customer service rep.

Using the previous example, take turns responding to the angry and irate customer. You certainly don't have to use our example case study; you can create one more specific to your own business, but the point is this: use the six simple rules noted earlier and you'll be in great shape to diffuse and deal with *any* irate customer.

FLIP THE SCRIPT: CASE STUDY

I was on the phone dealing with a customer service department. I went through the customary "button-mashing hell" to find the right person to talk to. My mind was already racing with thoughts of, "They shouldn't be telling me my call is important in a robot voice when they make it so damned hard to talk to somebody." Finally, I got somebody on the line and went over my issues. The customer service agent was summarizing what I'd told her into four points.

"Mr. Fleming, just to clarify, here's what we've agreed to today." She went through the points, and I interrupted her on the last point.

I made a minor correction on the fourth point. There was a short pause on the phone, and her immediate response was interesting. She said, *"You're absolutely right.* Thanks for correcting me," before continuing. She then re-iterated all four points, this time with the correct one at the end.

Call centers face people who will interrupt and correct them all the time. The reps are used to it. I've corrected them before and they've said, "Okay, sure." Other times, they've argued with me. But what surprised me was she thanked me for correcting her. She humanized the exchange and made me believe with her sincerity and words that she did want to help me as much as she could.

Here's the key lesson: it would have been easy to finish the call and mock their horrible system. It would have been comfortable to assume that they needed great customer service people on the phone because their company and products were so shoddy that they got a lot of calls. But that wouldn't have helped me make any real changes.

Instead of continuing to look for what they did wrong, I was able to find what they did right and find a way to improve both my company and the clients I helped to implement this practice.

It's easy to spot the failures in others and be glad that we're better. Similarly, it's easy to see our successes. But it's a lot more valuable to flip the script: look outside for ideas you can use to improve and look inside for criticisms to make.

A simple, powerful tool is that every time you read a story about a customer service situation that involves another company, ask how your people would handle a similar situation. You get bonus points for testing them on specific situations. Would they be prepared to deal with the angry customer? Would they have the language to diffuse a situation, or would they blow up, trying to pick a fight with your customer and end up in tomorrow's news? And if the client is really in the wrong, are your people prepared to deal with the situation?

Admitting When You're Wrong

This customer is not always right, but they're not always wrong, either.

Two key buzzwords thrown around in today's business world are authenticity and transparency. They're thrown around without much regard as to how companies can truly embrace these concepts when dealing with the challenging customers of our times. A colleague of mine, Steven Gaffney, is a renowned consultant and expert on the topic of honest communication. He's proposed a radical idea for the modern age: what if we adopted a policy of simple honesty with our customers as a critical tool in our arsenal that can lead to greater customer relations? It turns out that doing so can have a tremendously positive impact.

Whether the customer is right or wrong, it's up to you to be honest about it. If the customer is unhappy, disgruntled, dissatisfied, demanding, or disagreeable, it's up to us to figure out why and to know how to effectively respond. Today's customer wants to do business with the company that can say, "You know what, we were wrong. We messed up." They can smell a fake a mile away.

It's nearly impossible to act authentically as if the customer is right when you know they're downright wrong. Similarly, if the customer is right, but you're not willing to admit it, then we've got another problem.

In this exercise, we'll provide you with some tools to practice honest communications when dealing with difficult, demanding, and disagreeable customers.

In 2016, Wells Fargo was at the center of a major scandal. It was discovered that employees within the company were lying, cheating, and stealing from customers. (In the media frenzy that ensued after the fact, it was discovered that the pressures from upper management and the rigorous requirements for selling led customer-facing employees to engage in questionable activities, but that's a digression for another day.) If you or your company encourages a state of lies and deception, you'll eventually pay the price. Each of us makes the decision every day with our actions. Those of us dealing with customers have an ethical and moral duty to be as honest as possible with our customers. We want to show you how to do it as effectively as possible and continue to train your people to use honesty as a tool for dealing with the difficult customer (right or wrong!).

To practice admitting when you're wrong, try the following role-play. Use the role-play with your customer-facing people to learn and practice different ways to respond. One person should play the customer and another should play the business representative. After you've practiced it once, switch roles.

Role-Play: Overbooked Nightmare!

Business scenario: Imagine you're the front desk clerk at a small boutique bed and breakfast. You've just finished checking in your final room of the day. You're closing down your computer when you see a couple arriving and dragging their suitcases up the front steps. You're tired and just want to get home. You know that there's no vacancy and assume they must have the wrong hotel. They enter and immediately tell you they're tired after a long day of travel and want to check-in to their room quickly. He provides his last name. You have no record of the customer, and when the customer shows you his booking confirmation, it's evident to you that your company has made a mistake.

Customer scenario: You've just driven a long way to enjoy a fantastic weekend away with your spouse. You booked your room months ago and have been looking forward to this much-needed break for a while. The drive was long, but you and your spouse had a lot of fun. That being said, you're tired. It's time to check-in and chill out for a bit. You arrive to the inn and provide your name to the clerk. He seems confused and a bit frazzled. You were expecting more attentive service, given the price you were paying for this place. The front desk clerk finally informs you there's been some sort of mistake. He has no record of your booking, and they're totally full for the night.

Both participants should take turns playing both roles and attempt to come to different solutions, being as honest as possible without arguing with the customer. When it's your turn to be the customer, you might take a different approach. Will you get upset and angry, or will you be understanding? Try both.

Now, for fun, try it one more way. This time, suppose after a few minutes of searching, you've found the customer booked another date and showed up on the wrong weekend. The customer is tired, irate, and angry. How will you tell the customer he was wrong, being as honest as possible without trying to inflame the customer any further? Take turns in both roles.

After you've completed and taken turns, discuss and debrief what you learned from these simple role-play exercises. Was it harder than you expected to be honest when the customer was right or wrong? How did you resolve the situation? What could you have done differently?

The key lesson here is we don't always know how the customer will react, but if you can maintain your cool, be as authentic as possible, and attempt to resolve the solution as honestly as possible, then you've gone a long way in providing wonderful customer service.

What were your key learnings from this simple role-play? Was it harder than expected to be honest and authentic?

Part III

Chapter 8

How to Be Your Own Worst Customer

The Undercover Boss Syndrome

Shawn and I love the show *Undercover Boss.* Our favorite part of every episode is likely very different than most people. I know my wife gets a bit teary-eyed when the CEO rips off his mask and wig to show the troubled employees who he really is and then goes on to solve all their problems with a gift, a promotion, or a promise of change. We think that's all great and it makes us feel nice and cozy inside too, but that's definitely not our favorite part. Don't think we're heartless.

Shawn and I really love the moment the CEO returns to his boardroom. The table is made of gorgeous mahogany and it's glistening in the well-lit room. It's long and stereotypical of what you would expect in a typical boardroom. The executive team sits around the table, and they're exactly what you would expect as well. They're being paid out the wazoo, and they're getting ready to hear all of the great revelations their fearless leader learned in the first three days he spent in the field in the past 16 years. And, of course, it's shock and awe all around. The CEO explains he had no idea how bad things were out there. He tells them, "We've got a lot of work to do." The heads of his executive team nod in agreement as they sip their Starbucks coffees and watch the video recap of his experience. In the business world, this is referred to as the Ivory Tower Syndrome. Those who reside in the Ivory Tower are really out of touch with what's going on in the real world. This one scene in every episode really highlights just how out of touch with reality so many organizations are.

One of the fastest and easiest ways to counteract this tendency to ignore what's happening between your clients and your company is to implement and use the kind of customer issue reporting that we talked about in depth in Chapter 6. When you discipline yourself to look at what is causing your clients and your staff the most grief, week in and week out, it will be hard to ignore it for long.

The 90-Day Rule

It's easy to make a general point like we just have, and it's easy to nod your head along and think, "Yep, that makes sense!" We have never met anybody who disagrees with us when we say, "You know, it's really important that senior management gets their hands dirty on a regular basis to avoid the Undercover Boss pitfall."

On the other hand, we have met a lot of people who can't tell us the last time they dedicated time to investigating customer complaints directly. We have met a lot of people who don't know what the most common complaints their customers have are or even how to go about finding that information.

This disconnect is often referred to as the "knowing-doing gap." In short, it says that just knowing about something doesn't mean that you do it. It's the reason that intelligent people still smoke, avoid exercise, and overeat. It's also the reason that it's not enough for leaders to know what *should* happen; they also need to take action in order to make sure those things actually get done.

To that end, we often recommend a "90-day rule" be put in place for all managers and leaders in organizations who would not otherwise come into contact with clients or customers on a day-to-day basis.

The rule, in general, is this: never let more than 90 days go by without directly engaging with customer service in some capacity.

Maybe you dedicate a full day once per quarter to reviewing all the customer complaints that you've recorded for that quarter, and another day to work directly with your staff to create new ways to address the most common ones. Alternately, you might decide to dedicate an hour per week to a similar practice.

However you allocate the time, the recommendation is ultimately the same: don't let too much time go by without having a direct connection to your customer experiences. Ideally, you'll see both the positives and the negatives; you'll secret shop, you'll find and celebrate successes, and you'll build on strengths as well as identify weaknesses.

At the very least, you should be finding ways to dedicate the attention and resources required to help your people be able to help your clients more effectively on a continual basis.

What Even Your Angriest Customers Crave

There is a very old piece of advice in the world of direct marketing and face-to-face selling that is at the same time extremely obvious, simple, and almost universally overlooked. That piece of advice is *imagine every one of your prospects and customers is wearing a sign around their neck that says, "Make me feel special."*

This is the kind of advice that makes people very skeptical whenever they're on the customer side of the transaction. They worry that people are being insincere and trying to manipulate them into something that will serve the salesperson or the marketer, but will leave them in a worse position as a customer.

To be fair, they probably have a good reason to feel this fear. This is also the type of advice that certain types of marketers and salespeople use to cynically justify under-serving their clients. "Whatever I have to do or tell them to get them to buy is okay. I'm making them feel special in that moment, and that's worth the money!"

This, of course, is a gross mistreatment of the intent of this piece of advice. Or, if we want to be just as cynical as these salespeople, it is an accurate reading of the original intent, but it is not the best way to effectively and sustainably utilize this piece of advice.

Here is how we can use it ethically and effectively—both of which are required for a sustainable strategy.

A New Word for a Powerful Feeling

In 2012, John Koenig coined the word *sonder*. The definition is beautiful, and more importantly for this book, it is critical for effective customer service. Here is the definition of sonder:

The realization that each random passerby is living a life as vivid and complex as your own—populated with their own ambitions, friends, routines, worries and inherited craziness—an epic story that continues invisibly around you like an anthill sprawling deep underground, with elaborate passageways to thousands of other lives that you'll never know existed, in which you might appear only once, as an extra sipping coffee in the background, as a blur of traffic passing on the highway, as a lighted window at dusk.[1]

Making Them Feel Special Without Selling Your Soul

One of the not-so-hidden benefits of the role-playing training that we've advocated so heavily is that it forces you to see the world from the customer's point of view, especially in those situations where the customer is upset. It allows you to put the perspective of sonder into application as you start to look at the person across from you as a real person.

It is sometimes incredibly hard to do this, even though it sounds like the bare minimum for human interaction. It's really easy to become dismissive of those customers—to stop seeing them as individuals with real problems, issues, and complaints and instead to lump them all together into groups based on their complaint type.

"Oh, here's another Cheapo-Charles, whining about the price being too high."

"Can you believe it, another Late-Return Larry, telling us why the store policy shouldn't apply to him!"

"Here's Interrupting Irene, who won't let us finish telling her why she's wrong before she jumps in and starts yelling at us again!"

But when you're doing the role-playing training consistently, and putting in the effort to really put yourself into the shoes of the customer (like you did in the exercise in Chapter 7 about showing up at the hotel late at night to find there was no room), suddenly it becomes much easier to empathize with these people as people instead of representatives of their complaint class.

Why Most Customer Feedback Scores Are Useless

In 2003, Fred Reicheld, partner at Bain & Company, introduced the net promoter score (NPS).[2] NPS was introduced as a management tool that could help companies gauge and understand customer loyalty as it applied to revenue growth. The model was incredibly simple and became one of the most important tools for measuring customer loyalty. Customers of a company were asked a single question, using a 0–10 scale: how likely is it you would recommend (insert brand/company) to a friend or colleague? This is the official NPS question. Respondents were then grouped into categories such as:

- ☝ Promoters (score 9–10) are loyal enthusiasts who will keep buying and refer others, fueling growth.

- ☝ Passives (score 7–8) are satisfied but unenthusiastic customers who are vulnerable to competitive offerings.

- ☝ Detractors (score 0–6) are unhappy customers who can damage your brand and impede growth through negative word-of-mouth.

Subtracting the percentage of detractors from the percentage of promoters yields the net promoter score, which can range from a low of –100 (if every customer is detractor) to a high of 100 (if every customer is a promoter). NPS has long been hailed as the ultimate customer loyalty measurement tool, but in our opinion, it's a relatively useless tool. We have a slight suspicion it makes bigger brands and organizations feel good about their efforts because it takes an average look across all customers and how they're doing. If most are considered promoters, they must be doing something right. If more are passives, they know where to focus some efforts.

However, here are a few reasons why it's a relatively useless measurement. Some of the biggest reasons should be quite obvious. For example, it doesn't matter how many promoters you might have based on a single survey question. Unless you have referral programs and tools in place to encourage word-of-mouth, it means nothing. In essence, by looking at averages, it misses out on looking at one-to-one perspectives and experiences with a company as an opportunity to improvement. Even if 100 customers told a company their service was horrific and Johnny was a rotten account executive, they might not be willing to do anything about it because overall NPS scores are still averaging on the high end. Johnny continues to damage your company behind the scenes.

In mid-2016, in an interview with Bloomberg, Reicheld discussed how the single post-purchase follow-up survey had officially had its day, as companies merely bribed their customers by asking for 10s instead of using the survey as an opportunity to create improvement or meaningful change.[3] The employees didn't care what the customers had to say, so they bribed the customers to give top marks. Companies said things such as, "It would be really valuable for us if you gave us a 10." What good does that do to help you improve your customer's experience? Absolutely nothing. It's rather damaging because it signals to customers, "We don't really care if you're happy. We only care if we get high marks." In larger companies, there are huge investments made into adopting and using the NPS program, and then frontline employees bribe customers to give 10s. The scores end up as valuable as a bundle of Lehman Brothers stock.

The other huge issue, of course, is that the number means absolutely nothing unless you have the right processes in place to bring a customer back (such as active referral processes).

If you only ask one silly NPS question, how will you know where you're dropping the ball? How will you know where you need to improve and do a better job? How will you know where to invest your marketing dollars? How will you know how you're creating difficult, disgruntled, or dissatisfied customers?

It doesn't matter what customers say on a one-question survey. What matters is what they say to your front-line staff. What matters is what they say to their friends or family or if they're saying anything at all. A business full of 8s, 9s, and 10s doesn't mean squat. You can't get a true read on customers by what they say to this one question. The only thing that matters is what they actually do. As you'll see in a moment, in one of the most high-profile customer service incidents in the last 20 years, what the customers said they would do and what they actually did was worlds apart.

Is It Really So Bad to Punch Your Customers in the Face?

There are many possible approaches to dealing with disagreeable customers, each having its own particular set of pros and cons. In most cases, it is important to apologize to the customer and empathize with their situation. However, some people reading this will be in businesses where the threat of litigation is so high that any apology will be deemed as an admission of guilt, in which case this approach needs to be modified.

There is one approach that most experts agree is a sub-optimal solution: beating and bloodying the disagreeable customer while hundreds of others watch, some of them filming on their phones and uploading to social media.

United Airlines, ever a trailblazer in customer service techniques, used this approach in April 2017.[4]

On April 9th, 2017, Dr. David Dao and 130 other passengers flying to Louisville, Kentucky, boarded their plane and sat down. At some point after boarding, but before the flight took off, United decided that they needed to put four crew members on the plane to get them to the Louisville airport as well. Because the flight was at capacity, this would require them to kick four randomly selected passengers off the plane.

Dr. Dao was one of those passengers, but unlike the other three, he protested his removal, telling the United representatives that he had patients to see at his clinic in the morning.

After some argument, the United Airlines staff asked for assistance from the Department of Aviation security officers. As one account described it:

> Dao refused to leave his seat, and in the ensuing scuffle, he suffered injuries to his head and mouth when, according to another passenger, a security official threw him against the armrest before dragging him down the aisle by the arms, apparently unconscious.
>
> During the altercation, a number of passengers distressed by the incident voluntarily left

the aircraft. Four Republic Airline staff then sat in the vacated seats. Shortly afterwards, Dao managed to re-board the aircraft, repeatedly saying, "I have to go home." Eventually, he collapsed in a seat and was removed from the aircraft on a stretcher. The remaining passengers were then deplaned while blood from the scuffle was cleaned up.[5]

Dao's representatives report that he lost two teeth in the encounter, suffered a broken nose, and sustained damage to his sinuses—injuries requiring reconstructive surgeries to repair.

We share this story not to highlight a recommendation that you not injure your clients when they don't do what you want (but please don't injure your clients when they don't do what you want!). Instead, we want to share what we feel is one of the most interesting outcomes of this incident—namely, how much of a nonevent it turned out to be for United Airlines. Here is what happened during the next month:

- ♂ The case with Dr. Dao was settled fairly quickly for an undisclosed amount.

- ♂ Many more people shared their horror stories on United Airlines, and the media was thrilled to feature every new injustice.

- ♂ Countless groups polled individuals on social media and in real life, and consistently heard the same feedback: "Of course this will make us think twice about flying United! Of course we would fly on another airline, even if it means paying more for tickets! Of course we would fly on another airline, even if it means adding a three-hour layover!"

☃ Share prices rose about $6, adding $1.7 billion dollars to the valuation of United Airline stock.

It seems that all the negative attention and all the promises from people to avoid United amounted to... nothing. In fact, the company was seen as being 10 percent more valuable less than a month after the incident!

I'll admit that it seems odd for us to be highlighting the fact that this incident didn't really seem to harm United at all. It seems like an especially odd choice for a book about how to be better at customer service.

We bring it up because we think there are three key takeaways that any company can draw from this incident. (And please note, "It's okay to beat and bloody your clients" isn't one of them!)

1. Isolated negative incidents aren't the end of the world (even when they're highly publicized).

2. Never trust what people say on surveys.

3. You know what they say about publicity...

Isolated Negative Incidents Aren't the End of the World

As the old saying goes, "Pobody's nerfect." The bigger you get, the less able you will be to ensure that hundreds, thousands, or hundreds of thousands of employees will always act in the way you want them to.

From the customer side of the equation, you will be judged both against your own performance and that of your competitors. Luckily for United, airlines are pretty universally despised (except rare instances like Southwest Airlines, which has tied its identity to having great customer service and carefully managing the expectations gap to a T).

Of course, we're not suggesting that it's not worth investing in developing better customer service—we'd be crazy to do that! What we want to point out here, though, is that you can fail about as hard as it's possible to fail, and it is not necessarily the end of the world.

From the company side, a strong and well-communicated corporate culture helps everybody in the organization to recognize what's expected of them, and creating an environment where people have pride in their work ensures they want to live up to the ideals of that corporate culture.

The stories that are told about a company are very different depending on who is telling them. Longtime and loyal customers will tell stories about when the company went above and beyond. Angry customers and the media will tell stories about when the company fails. It is up to company leaders to tell both kinds of stories and to ensure that everybody knows which stories they want to be part of.

Never Trust What People Say on Surveys

Surveys are dangerous, and they've never been more dangerous than now. Although we can communicate with any of our prospects or customers at almost no cost, making sense of that communication is almost impossible.

Almost half of the people surveyed about the United incident said they'd pay more money and accept a layover to avoid traveling with United, and yet their passenger rates only climbed in the month after the incident.

People routinely say they'd recommend the service to a friend (the standard question that makes up the net promoter score measurement), and yet for most companies, there is no relationship between this score and the actual number of referrals generated.

More boycotts are started and "liked" on social media than are possible to count, and yet the net impact to the companies involved is negligible.

The somewhat complicated explanation for all of this is that *people lie.*

They may not even know they're lying when they do it. They may genuinely believe that their future selves will boycott the mean company they read a negative story about. But when push comes to shove, when it's time to pull out the wallets and make a decision, those feelings go away, and instead they do what they've always done.

You Know What They Say About Publicity...

The fact that bad publicity doesn't hurt a company's profit margin doesn't mean that companies with bad customer service are off the hook. It just means that people will rely on their own experiences and history with the company rather than rage-quitting based on negative publicity.

So, what happens when their personal history becomes littered with negative experiences? What happens when bad customer service isn't a notable and newsworthy exception and isn't "industry-standard bad" but is, instead, consistently bad and consistently worse than the industry average?

In short, what happens when an individual customer has enough bad experiences that they decide it's not worth doing business with you anymore? Then (and only then) will you start to see the negative consequences of having horrible policies and bad people in place.

Don't worry about what people say in surveys. Don't worry about what you see in the media. But pay close, detailed, regular, and meticulous attention to the negative experiences that customers are actually having and find ways to reduce them.

Sometimes that means that you'll need to change your policies to stop being inconvenient to your customers. Sometimes it means giving entire locations or regions additional training (and of course monitoring the behavior change created by that training to ensure the new behaviors are sticking). Sometimes it means firing employees or managers if they are consistently unable to bring their performance up to the minimum standard.

But mostly, it means that you have to decide that you're going to put your time and energy into serving your customers better and not just issuing decrees to that effect (or spending money on systems and methods that promise no-effort results, hoping that solves the problem).

Scary Math

We were working with a company a few years back that was in the retail space and helping them to improve the consistency of their customer experiences.

At first, the client wasn't convinced that they needed any work in this area. "We've run internal studies and found that our people operate the way we expect between 90 and 95 percent of the time, which makes it very unlikely that any customer will have a bad experience, and if they do, it puts the odds of them having two bad experiences in a row at almost 0."

Many companies that we've worked with since have expressed similar sentiments. Consider the customer-facing portions of your business. Would you say that you ensure your customers walk away happy 90, 95, 99 percent or more of the time? If so, you may be convinced that there's nothing to worry about.

It was exactly this kind of complacency that our client had. In order to demonstrate the seriousness of every negative interaction (even if they happened less than 5 percent of the time), we developed a simulation to show them the effects of various levels of consistency. What we share next is almost verbatim what we shared with them.

Consider a company where customers purchase, on average, once every two months, and where the average customer lifetime is approximately three years.

That means you can expect 18 purchase interactions with each customer. If you are perfect 90 percent of the time, that 10 percent lapse means that almost every customer will have at least one and probably two experiences at minimum where something is very inconsistent.

In working with a client a few years back, we created a computer simulation to show the impact of this inconsistency. Look, we were using a computer to do this, so bear with us. You don't need to know the math inside and out, just bear with it. It works and illustrates the key learning points perfectly. It started with the following rules:

- A company has 100,000 customers.

- Each customer has 18 interactions.

- Each interaction has a 90 percent likelihood of being good, and a 10 percent likelihood of being inconsistent enough to upset the customer.

⚬ If a customer has five good interactions after a bad interaction, they "forget" the bad one. Otherwise, if a customer has more than two bad experiences without five good ones to wipe the slate, the customer will leave.

In short, we're saying, "We are amazing 90 percent of the time!" So, what are the odds that a customer leaves?

With these numbers, 62,000 of your customers will leave at some point before the "normal" lifespan of 18 purchases. If we adjust things so that 95 percent of their experiences are stellar, and only 5 percent are cause for concern, still 33,000 of your customers will leave. If we're incredible, and 99 percent of the time we give great service, then we'll still lose about 6,300 customers. Suppose every customer had a lifetime value of $5,000 and you lost 62,000 of them. Now you can do some scary math!

Of course, this is just an illustration with a very specific set of assumptions. Within your customer base, there may be a higher or lower tolerance for negative experiences, but it is certainly worth taking the time to consider how even very minor variations can create a very major negative customer impact.

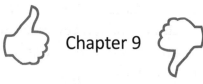

Chapter 9

The Customer Success Toolkit

The Rosetta Stone of Customer Service

A quick Amazon.com search for the words "customer service" yields 1,194,439 books on the topic at the time of writing this one. If that's surprising, it shouldn't be, especially if you've read this far into the book. Pleasing the customer (whether they're good, bad, or unhappy) is critical to the success of any organization.

It's been said that by the year 2020, companies will spending more than $83 billion per year on outsourcing their customer service activities.[1] We think that's just crazy. Big organizations outsource customer service to places with cheap labor and provide cheap, lousy service. This only adds to customer unhappiness and feelings of ill-intent toward brands. We've shared various examples throughout the book where the customer and the call are not really that important to anyone. And let's be honest, the call might be recorded, but they're not using those calls to improve or perform. To sum it up, for the love of all that is holy in this world, never ever outsource the "satisfaction" of your clients to a department without a sales, profit, or loss responsibility.

"Your Complaint Is Stupid!" Determining the Validity of Complaints

We seem to have this desire to turn customer service and the art of managing our reputations into something way more than it is. The more than one million books on Amazon are great proof of that. But I've prided myself on helping my clients demystify customer service and respond to customers offline, online, and anywhere in between. When we work with our clients' customer service, support, and social media teams to foster brand loyalty and address customer concerns, we want to train them to simply answer the following question when dealing with a customer:

Is this complaint, comment, feedback, or review valid or invalid?

Here are some examples and fictitious reviews we've created for the purpose of this book to help illustrate the point. The goal here is to *always* first determine if the review, feedback, or complaint is valid or invalid. Let's define what each means. A valid customer concern means exactly that. The customer has every right to be upset, angry, confused, or unhappy. An invalid customer concern is on the opposite end of the spectrum. For whatever reason, the complaint may be legitimate and the customer may genuinely be unhappy, but it's invalid. Now don't worry, we're not going to tell these people to get lost. We're still going to respond in a way that helps us alleviate the customer's problem in the most beneficial way possible, but we're going to do it in a way that's smart, simple, and works every time.

Let's suppose you're in charge of your company's online reputation (which is another point in itself; you really don't have an online or offline reputation—you have a reputation, but bear with me here). Read the two fictitious reviews I've created to illustrate our main point here and tell me if each one is valid or invalid.

Review #1

We just got back from a visit to New York City where we stayed at the W Hotel in Times Square. This hotel was absolutely awful. We went to bed early because we had an early flight the next day, but neither my wife nor I could sleep. The room was bright and loud all night long. It looked as if the hotel had tried to add blackout curtains to block all the lights, but it didn't help. I asked the front desk what they intended to do about our stay. We weren't offered anything. No free night, no free meal, nothing! My wife and I had the worst sleep of our lives. We were exhausted and when we had to leave at 7 a.m., it was super busy in this area already! Needless to say, we'll never be back.

Would you say this review is valid or invalid? Before you answer, let's look at one more and then talk about each.

Review #2

We just got back from our stay at the supposedly "exquisite and five-star luxury" Fleming Bed & Breakfast in the mountains of North Carolina. We paid $749 for one night. The cost isn't the issue. Hotels like this usually cost this, but our bed wasn't even made when we checked in. There was a laundry basket left in our room. There was a teenage girl working the front door who really wasn't doing much. Needless to say, we won't be going back. It's unfortunate; we had such high expectations for this place!

How about this review—is it valid or invalid?

The first is invalid. Staying in the heart of Times Square, in New York City, comes with some degree of understanding that you're spending a night in the greatest city in the world, in the city that never sleeps, and in the heart of the planet (Times Square). That's not to say a guest isn't entitled to a good night's sleep, but the complaint/review is invalid and needs to be dealt with as so.

The second complaint is valid. Anyone staying in a room that costs $749 per night in a hotel that's marketed to customers as "exquisite and five-star luxury" deserves an experience that closely matches those expectations. The key to all of this is the customer expectations you've created about your products and services.

After determining if it's valid, we put it through three more steps. So, the total cycle looks like this:

1. Is it valid or invalid?

2. Does it come from an actual customer?

3. What is the likely consequence of not addressing it in a meaningful way?

4. What is an appropriate response, both internally and externally? (What are you going to do to fix it, and how are you going to let others know you've fixed it?)

In April of 2017, there was a minor marketing flub on the part of Pepsi that caused a stir for a few hours. They had aired an ad that bore some resemblance to a famous scene from a clash between a protester and police at a Black Lives Matter protest. Pepsi's message, according to their PR team afterward, stated that they were "Trying to project a global a message of unity, peace and understanding."

Social media was ablaze with posts bashing Pepsi, which fueled blogs and online content aggregators with stories about the "huge and costly" blunder that Pepsi had made, and even what's left of the respectable news organizations all had pieces talking about it. At best, critics pointed out it was tone-deaf. At worst, it was exploitative and attempting to subvert a social movement for the purpose of selling more sugar water.

Let's pass it through the four steps:

1. Is the complaint valid or invalid?

    Yes, by any objective measure, the complainers have a point here. It was in poor taste, and it was a mistake. I can't imagine anybody inside or outside Pepsi arguing anything else.

2. Does it come from an actual customer?

    This is an interesting question. At first blush, it would seem apparent that obviously it came from a customer. It came from thousands of customers who were posting on social media!

    Let's dive a little deeper into this question before we pass over this step, though. Who are Pepsi's customers? The easy answer is "You, me, and Billy McGee! We're all Pepsi's customers!" But that's not really the best answer, is it?

    You, me, and Billy don't order our Pepsi directly from the corporation. We don't call up the Pepsi hotline every time we want a drink of their delightful beverages. We head to a grocery store, a restaurant, a vending machine or a gas station, and we buy Pepsi from an intermediary entity.

    So, it stands to reason that Pepsi's true customers are those intermediate entities (and even there, it's not the individual stores, restaurants, or gas stations, but rather their purchasing departments). Complaints from those groups would constitute a complaint from a customer. You, me, and Billy are, at best, customers of their customers, and it would take a lot of us taking very massive and coordinated action to even be noticed by the good folks at Pepsi's accounting department.

3. What is the likely consequence of not addressing it in a meaningful way?

   At this stage, we have a valid complaint that did not come from a customer. What are the risks of doing nothing? To do this, we'll consider some facts about Pepsi consumption.

   About 3,405,750 gallons of Pepsi are sold in the United States alone every day.[2] That's the equivalent of about 36,315,980 cans every day of the year. And that, of course, is only the sales of Pepsi Cola. Add in the other popular beverages sold by Pepsi (Mountain Dew, Diet Pepsi, Sierra Mist, etc.) and the number triples to a little more than 110,000,000 cans per day.

   So let's assume that the anti-Pepsi social media crowd is effective at reaching 10,000,000 people and convincing 1 percent of them to give up Pepsi for a full week (a much greater impact than most social media campaigns have, but we're trying to be a little alarmist here). The national soft drink consumption average in the United States is about 1.3 cans per day, so to give the movement extra credit, we'll round upward to 2.

What's the total impact? Two cans per day × 7 days × 100,000 people = 1.4 million fewer cans sold.

The entirety of the impact, even given wildly optimistic assumptions about people's actual behavior, would equate to about 1.3 percent of one day's sales in the United States alone. The more likely impact, of course, is nothing.

4. What is an appropriate response, both internally and externally?

In this case, it's screamingly obvious that the appropriate response is simply to issue a vague apology through your PR department, and then let it blow over (which is exactly what Pepsi did). To give it any more attention externally would only be to do the protesters' jobs for them, at no benefit to anybody.

Internally, they may need to have a word with their marketing teams, expand the diversity of their focus groups, create better processes for moving advertising through the "concept leads to validation leads to release" phases, and generally try to avoid being hugely insensitive in the future. But make no mistake—given the relatively minor stakes and potential consequences, it would be a very large misstep for any executive to spend too much time worrying about this. After all, there are innumerable things they can do to positively impact their relationships with their core clients. Spending too much time focusing on the complaints of their customers' customers would be wildly counterproductive.

Of course, this same four-step process is also one that you can go through on the front lines, dealing with a specific complaint from an angry customer in front of you.

During your role-playing training, you should be aware of all four of these elements. Structure some role-plays that have valid complaints and others that have invalid complaints. In most settings, especially face to face, step 2 will be very easy. It is almost a certainty that you will be dealing with an actual customer. It is only when you enter the murky world of online reputation management that you really must make the distinction between customer and noncustomer.

In real-world interactions, setting aside online reviews and public relation concerns for a moment, step 3 shifts subtly from "What is the likely consequence of not addressing it in a meaningful way?" to "What are the consequences of not resolving this now?" Frontline customer service always has the option of saying, "I understand your position, and I would really love to help you, but unfortunately my hands are tied here. I will have to get my manager involved, and that can't happen until tomorrow. If you leave me your contact information, I will make sure she gets in touch with you tomorrow."

Sometimes, this is exactly what is needed. It provides a cooling-off period for the customer, which is especially valuable if they believe you truly do have their best interest at heart and are advocating on their behalf. At the same time, it gives your team some time to figure out how far you are willing to go to resolve the issue.

On the other hand, overuse of this tactic can backfire quickly. Your customers aren't stupid, and if they get the sense that you are stalling for time, or really have no interest in helping them, then the delay will only serve to solidify their position and make it harder for them to walk away feeling respected and valued.

We've talked a lot about bad service so far. I want to finish with a story about the best service I ever had.

The Best Service I Ever Received and How You Can Provide It Too

I was working at LinkedIn/Lynda.com's offices in Santa Barbara, California, shooting a course for them on creating lifelong, loyal customers. My colleague, the esteemed author and consultant Roberta Matuson happened to be in town at the same time. We decided to grab dinner one night, and a restaurant came highly recommended. We were told the restaurant was hidden up in the hills of Montecito, and it was not to be missed.

We found the San Ysidro Ranch and were seated at an outdoor table. Our server, James, approached us. He introduced himself and promptly offered to get us drinks. He asked what we liked and immediately made suggestions that suited us perfectly. He was polite, but not obsequious. He was knowledgeable about the menu, but more importantly about helping us match our tastes and mood to what was on offer. In short, within the first 60 seconds of sitting down, James had made an impression unlike any other server I'd ever met.

James returned with our drinks and began to carefully, slowly, and enthusiastically explain all the evening's specials. I was entranced listening to him describe the evening's signature dishes. But then James stopped and asked us a simple question: "What are you in the mood for this evening?" Again, not a strange question, but it was James's responses that caught us off guard. He went on to make fantastic suggestions. He made recommendations of dishes we could share, and suggested what would and wouldn't pair well together. Of course, being the brilliant consultants that we are, we followed his advice to the letter and had an unforgettable meal.

We've all had great service and we've all had subpar and even terrible service. But I've never had service that was comparable to this. It quite literally redefined my standard metric of what "service" means, not just in a restaurant context, but in how I work with my clients and in how I will help guide them to work with theirs.

It's hard to describe the essence of James and what was going on, but Roberta and I noticed it quickly. There was something special going on here. So, we asked him to tell us the secret, and his answer floored us.

James told us the story of growing up in his father's fine dining restaurant in Mexico. He said it was one of the only "fine" dining establishments in the area. He explained that he owed everything to his father for teaching him that the guests he was serving at that very moment had to be treated as the most important people in his life.

If he had told me this at the start of our experience, I would have rolled my eyes! But the passion within James was undeniable, and he made us feel it.

I do a lot of work with organizations on improving the customer experience and building stronger customer relationships, and there's a tried and true universal law that we can use in almost any business, in any industry, regardless of the situation:

Do everything within your power to make the current customer feel special.

It doesn't have to be anything big. Just make the customer feel special. Better yet, imagine every customer who walks into your world has a big neon sign above their head that says, "Make me feel special."

There are a lot of things you could and should do in your company that are dependent on time, effort, or capital. There are countless strategies you could employ that are a gamble. But there's nothing stopping you and everybody in your company from finding ways to make your clients feel more special.

Challenge: Do something today—even just one thing—that makes a current customer feel special. Here's the most important part: you need to believe it yourself. If you're just doing it because it's your job, the customer will smell it a mile away. If you have one James in your business, you are incredibly lucky.

If everybody in your business was even half as good as James, you would be unstoppable. So, what's stopping you?

Final Thoughts

We started this book by talking about a 60-year-old piece of research that shed light on how quickly people can form bonds with one another and, more importantly, see others as enemies. We've looked at individual stories and studies to demonstrate how this impacts us in a very real way, every day of our lives. If you're like any of the people who were kind enough to read early drafts of this book, you found yourself thinking of times that you were irrationally angry, upset, or disappointed with companies you've done business with, and you developed a slightly more compassionate view of your most troublesome customers.

By visiting Lake Wobegon and the Bizarro World and learning that it's not enough to mask yourself with lemon juice before robbing a bank, we hope you've developed a healthy skepticism about your initial diagnoses of what the "real problem" with difficult customers is.

Our tour of sales processes and the expectations gap gave us an insight into the genesis of many negative customer experiences, and it hopefully sparked many ideas about how to minimize the gap between the experience as a prospect and as a client.

We cannot overstate the importance of the tools introduced in Part 2 of this book. The adoption of script books, internal benchmarking tools, and regular role-playing training can transform the way your company works with your most difficult customers and, more importantly, they can help you avoid creating those difficult customers in the first place. Did we mention these tools always drive increased revenues and profits? Always.

We hope you came away with new ways to make your customers feel special on a consistent basis. Remember, it's better to be consistently good than intermittently great. Put the tools and ideas in this book to use in your company and you'll see a marked difference in both the frequency and the outcome of negative customer incidents.

Finally, reach out! It can be hard to go from reading a concept to creating real change in any company. We have built processes, tools, and strategic programs with the sole purpose of transforming the customer service capabilities of organizations, and we've seen the tremendous impact such programs can have. Email us at noah@noahfleming.com and set up a call with both of us to discover how we can do the same for you.

Notes

Introduction

1. "Stupid travel complaints," *Toronto Star*, September 2011, *https://thestar.com/life/travel/2011/09/16/stupid_travel_complaints.html*.

2. Peter Drucker, *Concepts of the Corporation* (New York: John Day Company, 1946).

Chapter 1

1. Muzafer Sherif, O.J. Harvey, B. Jack White, William R. Hood, and Caroyln W. Sherif, *Intergroup Conflict and Cooperation: The Robbers Cave Experiment* (Norman: University Book Exchange, 1961).

2. Ibid.

3. Drew Westen, et al. "An fMRI study of motivated reasoning: Partisan political reasoning in the U.S. presidential election," Atlanta, GA: Emory University, Psychology Department (2006).

4. John Kenneth Galbraith, *Economics, Peace and Laughter* (New York: New American Library, 1971), 50.

5. Thomas Gilovich, *How We Know What Isn't So: The Fallibility of Human Reason in Everyday Life*, https://goodreads.com/work/quotes/121184.

6. Michael Basch, *Customer Culture: How FedEx and Other Great Companies Put the Customer First Every Day* (Pearson Education, 2002).

Chapter 2

1. Robert Famighetti, *The World Almanac and Book of Facts 1996* (St. Martin's Press, 1995).

2. Ola Svenson, "Are We All Less Risky and More Skillful Than Our Fellow Drivers?" *Acta Psychologica*, February 1981, 47 (2): 143–148.

3. K. Patricia Cross, "Not Can But Will College Teachers Be Improved?" *New Directions for Higher Education*, Spring 1977 (17): 1–15.

4. Mark D. Alicke and Olesya Govorun, "The Better-Than-Average Effect." In Mark D.

Alicke, David A. Dunning, and Joachim I. Krueger, *The Self in Social Judgment* (Psychology Press, 2005), 85–106.

5. Aaron Crowe, "24% Of Drivers Admit To Coming Close To Causing An Accident While Texting," *http://cheapcarinsurance.net/24-of-drivers-admit-to-coming-close-to-causing-an-accident-while-texting.*

6. "Bizarro World," *https://en.wikipedia.org/wiki/Bizarro_World.*

Chapter 3

1. Martin Seligman, *Authentic Happiness: Using the New Positive Psychology to Realize Your Potential for Lasting Fulfillment* (New York: Free Press, 2002).

Chapter 4

1. Tony Hsieh, *Delivering Happiness: A Path to Profits, Passion, and Purpose* (New York: Grand Central Publishing, 2010).

Chapter 5

1. Atul Gawande, *The Checklist Manifesto* (New York: Metropolitan Books, 2009).

2. It's a fun film worth watching. Learn more at *https://en.wikipedia.org/wiki/The_Big_Kahuna* (film) or *http://imdb.com/title/tt0189584.*

3. Hermann Ebbinghaus, "Memory: A Contribution to Experimental Psychology," trans. H. Ruger and C. Bussenius (New York: Teachers College, 1913).

Chapter 8

1. "Sonder," *http://dictionaryofobscuresorrows.com/post/23536922667/sonder.*

2. See *http://netpromotersystem.com/about.*

3. Jennifer Kaplan, "The Inventor of Customer Satisfaction Surveys Is Sick of Them, Too," *https://bloomberg.com/news/articles/2016-05-04/tasty-taco-helpful-hygienist-are-all-those-surveys-of-any-use.*

4. Matthew Diebel, "United Airlines passenger David Dao was violent before removal, aviation police say," *https://usatoday.com/story/news/nation/2017/04/25/united-david-dao-police-report-dragging-incident/100873730.*

5. "United Express Flight 3411 incident," *https://en.wikipedia.org/wiki/United_Express_Flight_3411_incident.*

Chapter 9

1. Jack Loechner, "Poor Customer Service Cost Companies $83 Billion Annually," *https://mediapost.com/publications/article/122502/poor-customer-service-costs-companies-83-billion.html.*

2. "Coke Vs. Pepsi: By The Numbers," *http://nasdaq. com/article/coke-vs-pepsi-by-the-numbers-cm337909.*

Index

About the Authors

Noah Fleming is a sought-after business strategy consultant, speaking and best-selling author. His landmark books, *Evergreen* and *The Customer Loyalty Loop*, break new ground on customer loyalty, customer service, customer experience, and customer retention. His firm, Fleming Consulting & Co., has helped companies ranging from several million to over $5 billion in annual revenues exploit new opportunities and correct costly oversights. He is routinely quoted and mentioned in publications like *Forbes*, *Entrepreneur Magazine* and more. Noah is a sought-after speaker, with notable engagements at SXSW, Hubspot's Inbound, a talk at Google's HQ in New York City, and numerous schools and professional trade associations (including a TEDx talk viewed by thousands of people). Fleming publishes his weekly newsletter, The Tuesday Tidbit, for over 30,000 readers. Find out more at NoahFleming.com.

For the past 15 years, **Shawn Veltman** has worked alongside Noah to develop unique intellectual property, tools, and applications successfully implemented in hundreds of companies across dozens of industries. Veltman has been involved with companies ranging from Internet start-ups to medical device manufacturers, helping executives extract world-class performances from their sales and marketing teams. Shawn and Noah also record and publish a valuable 15-minute weekly podcast called *The Evergreen Show* available on iTunes.

ALSO BY NOAH FLEMING: *THE CUSTOMER LOYALTY LOOP*

> "*The Customer Loyalty Loop* is a fun, easy to read, yet science-based look at all things customer-related. Put Noah Fleming's advice to work, and learn how to identify customers, win them over, and keep them coming back for more."
> —**Daniel H. Pink**, author of *To Sell Is Human*

OTHER BUSINESS BOOKS FROM THE PUBLISHER